Personal Origins

The Report of a Working Party
on Human Fertilisation and Embryology
of the Board for Social Responsibility

Second Revised Edition

Church House Publishing
Church House
Great Smith Street
London SW1P 3NZ

Church House Publishing
Church House
Great Smith Street
London SW1P 3NZ

ISBN 0 7151 6581 X

Published for the Board for Social Responsibility of the General Synod of the Church of England by Church House Publishing

1st edition 1985
2nd revised edition 1996

Printed in England by Longdunn Press Ltd

Contents

Foreword to second edition

Personal Origins was first published in 1985. It represented a considered response to and reflection on the ethical and theological questions raised by contemporary developments in the ability to alleviate human infertility.

Since 1985, there have been new developments in assisted conception techniques and the enactment of legislation to regulate their use. This revised edition of *Personal Origins* takes account both of the new possibilities for treatment and also the consequences of the Human Fertilisation and Embryology Act 1990.

The Board is indebted to the Revd Dr Mary Seller for her very careful work in updating the factual content of the report. The remainder of the text is as it was in the first edition, though there have been some minor changes to clarify meaning. References to proposals in the 'Warnock' Report (published in 1984) have been omitted now that the legislation has been published. Finally, Appendix II has been revised to include recent publications that also belong in a list of helpful background literature.

The aim of the exercise has been to update and so extend the useful life of a report which has been valued and found useful by many in the Church. In the intervening decade since its first publication there has been continuing discussion of the relationship between humanity and nature but the moral argument presented in the report retains its validity.

In producing this second edition, there has been consultation with the other members of the Working Party, particularly with Professor R. J. Berry, and the text has been discussed twice and amended by the Board's Science, Medicine and Technology Committee.

October 1996   ✠ RICHARD OXON

Chairman
Board for Social Responsibility

Foreword to first edition

When the Warnock Committee on Human Fertilisation and Embryology was formed in 1982, the Board was fortunate in being able to find from within its own membership the knowledge and expertise required to enable it to submit evidence by the required date of March 1983. Professor R. J. Berry (Professor of Genetics, University College, London), Dr Mary Seller (Reader in Developmental Genetics at the United Medical School of Guy's and St Thomas' Hospitals, London), and the Revd Professor Keith Ward (Professor of Moral and Social Theology, King's College, London), together with the Board Secretary, Prebendary John Gladwin, were invited to undertake this task as far back as October 1982; and the Revd Professor Oliver O'Donovan (Regius Professor of Moral and Pastoral Theology in the University of Oxford) with whom the Working Party was in active corre-spondence, was invited formally to join the group in January 1983.

The Working Party reported to the Board that the submission of evidence to the Warnock Committee should mark the beginning rather than the end of its labours. The advent of new medical techniques in the field of human fertilisation and embryology had produced new problems which not merely raised ethical issues but which also required theological elucida-tion. Accordingly the Board encouraged the Working Party to do further work along these lines and approved its new terms of reference:

> To consider recent and potential developments in medicine and science related to human fertilisation and embryology; to consider the theological and moral issues raised by such developments; and to advise the Board for Social Respons-ibility on the response that the Church of England ought to be making.

The Working Party met 15 times, two of them residential. It spent longer on its labours than was foreseen, for three reasons. First, its members were having to tackle novel issues for which there were no precedents in the whole history of moral theology. Second, the Working Party discovered fundamental differences of approach among its members which prevented unanimity. Thirdly, its work was interrupted by the need to approve the Board's official response to the Warnock Report before the end of 1984.

The final report not only describes new (as well as potential future) medical techniques in this field, but it also addresses itself to matters of ethical principles and judgements. It also concerns itself with the theology of marriage, and the theology of the human embryo, together with questions concerning human dominion and pastoral theology, so far as these are relevant to these issues. It reveals clearly how differences of theological and ethical approach will result in differing conclusions.

The Board, in expressing its gratitude to the members of the Working Party, hopes that the report will be widely read, and that it will help its readers toward a deeper understanding of, and a more informed judgement about these difficult new choices which medical technology has thrust upon us.

March 1985   ✠ HUGH BIRMINGHAM

Chairman
Board for Social Responsibility

Introduction

1.   In November 1982 the Government set up a Committee of Inquiry into Human Fertilisation and Embryology under the chairmanship of Dame Mary Warnock. The Board for Social Responsibility submitted evidence on behalf of the General Synod of the Church of England.[1] In preparing this evidence it became clear that there was a need to bring together the threads of moral theology that are relevant to Anglican thinking on the subject, and to apply these to the apparently new problems raised by the scientific developments considered by the Warnock Committee. Accordingly, the Board appointed a Working Party consisting of two moral theologians, a social theologian, an experimental biologist, and a geneticist to prepare a report setting out the possible Christian responses to these problems. Some of the work of this group was contained in the Board's formal response to the Government in November 1984.[2] *Personal Origins* goes further, presenting the principles behind this response, placing them in a general framework rather than as comments on the specific proposals of the Warnock Committee. In some ways it was an extension and amplification of the issues discussed in a report of a Free Church Federal Council/BCC Working Party, chaired by the Very Revd Peter Baelz, *Choices in Childlessness*, 1982.

2.   The Human Fertilisation and Embryology Act 1990 (HFE Act) was the parliamentary response to the Warnock Committee report and subsequent discussion. It was implemented in 1991. It placed assisted conception techniques and human embryo research under statutory control, and reflected many of the recommendations in the first edition of *Personal Origins*. While the underlying moral issues and theological considerations are unchanged, the Board felt that *Personal Origins* should be updated with respect to the Act and to developments since it was first published in 1985. This has now been done in this second edition. The basic text remains unaltered but matters of fact have been amended as appropriate.

3.   In setting out the relevant principles, we have sought to apply Biblical understanding and Christian ethical tradition in the light of scientific knowledge. Some issues remain contentious; others are not capable

1

of resolution at the moment and for these we have set out the different possible interpretations. In doing this, we have submerged our personal and various viewpoints in the recognition that different but seemingly valid Christian conclusions can be drawn from the available data, while acknowledging that the implications of these conclusions are often very distinct.

4.   We have identified three major areas of debate:

(a)   The status of the fertilised human egg or early embryo, and the protection it should be given (Chapter 3);

(b)   The nature of the marriage bond, and the effect on it of the introduction of a third (or even fourth) party in artificial insemination by donor (DI), ovum donation etc. (Chapter 4);

(c)   The nature and extent of divine providence and human responsibility (Chapter 2).

5.   In addition, we have taken note of the pastoral problems and counselling needs arising from the implementation (or refusal) of the technological developments.

6.   We have had most difficulty in our search to describe and define the status of the human embryo. Many Christians believe that the same protection should be accorded to the newly fertilised egg as to a postnatal human being. This belief is based on the recognition that the unique genetic complement of an individual is largely established at conception (although see Paragraphs 86–7) and that there is no obvious threshold in embryonic development to form the traditional distinction between an 'unformed' and a 'formed' foetus. However, for at least 14 days after conception, embryos may divide (to form twins) or even fuse, and thus it seems that individuality is not established until that time, at least in those cases. Even the authoritative Roman Catholic statement (1974) on abortion acknowledges:

> This Declaration deliberately leaves aside at what moment in time the spiritual soul is infused. On this matter tradition is not unanimous and writers differ.[3]

7.   The Warnock Committee itself asserted that:

> although the questions of when life or personhood begin appear to be questions of fact susceptible of straightforward answers, we hold that the answers to such questions in fact are complex amalgams of factual and moral judgement. Instead of trying to answer these questions directly we have therefore gone straight to the question of how it is right to treat the embryo.[4]

The Committee was criticised for this decision on the ground that it avoided the key issue. They recognised the importance of the question but did not address themselves to it directly. Notwithstanding they:

> agreed that the embryo of the human species ought to have a special status and that no one should undertake research on human embryos the purposes of which could be achieved by the use of other animals or in some other way. The status of the embryo is a matter of fundamental principle ....[5]

8.   We have tried to establish the reasons for maintaining a special status for the human embryo with only limited success. Biology, scripture and tradition give only partial answers, while the often-used concepts of 'person'[6] and 'potential'[7] do not help very much. As the Roman Catholic commentator John Mahoney SJ notes:

> perhaps the most ambiguous term in the entire discussion is that of 'person', which can mean very different things to different people .... (For many) the idea of person (as existing from the fertilisation of the ovum) has moved so far from ordinary usage and becomes so attenuated and blurred, so distanced from its ordinary understanding as to be now altogether meaningless, and indeed misleading. The most such people are disposed to concede is that which exists from the moment of fertilisation is something which contains the potential to develop into a human person, but which is not yet a person, on any normal understanding of that word.

Others argue that while the conceptus cannot be said to manifest the activities of a human person, nevertheless it:

3

already possesses the endowments of a human person so that rather than speak of a potential human person one should more correctly speak of a human person with potential.

The debate, however, is not clarified by introducing the idea of potential, since its use on both sides simply reflects and extends the previous fundamental positions. Those who would argue that to describe the conceptus as only potentially a human person is to ignore the fact that even the child at birth is still only potentially a human person and are using the term 'potential' to mean the capacity to become more of a person, or more fully a person, in terms of characteristically personal activities. While on the other hand, those who claim that this description of a potential human person applies exclusively to the embryo or foetus at an early stage are using the term 'potential' to mean that it is not yet in any real sense a person at all.[8]

9.   Other language used to describe the status of the foetus is that of 'rights', often contrasting the 'right' of the mother with the 'right' to life. We have not found this helpful. Scripture does not use such concepts, but speaks instead of responsibilities or duties and their associated privileges.

10.   We are aware that the conclusions some of us have drawn about DI or ovum donation (and hence the nature of the marriage bond) differ from previous Anglican pronouncements. Those who hold this view see the use of third-party gametes by an infertile couple as a positive affirmation of the family. Nevertheless this is another area where a range of views is held by members of the Working Party and these are set out in Chapter 4.

11.   After the publication of the Warnock Report there was much discussion about the need for legislation to regulate assisted conception techniques and other embryo-related procedures. After wide consultation this culminated in the Human Fertilisation and Embryology Act 1990, passed in Parliament with a general recognition that a regulating authority was a better mechanism than ministerial control for controlling clinical practice and furthering ethical debate.

12.   The HFE Act governs the production of human embryos outside the body, and their subsequent development and usage. The Act further controls the use of donated gametes, prohibits certain practices in connection with embryos and gametes, and it established the Human Fertilisation and Embryology Authority (HFEA). The Act explicitly states 'that a woman may not be provided with treatment services unless account has been taken of the welfare of any child who may be born as a result of the treatment (including the need of that child for a father), and of any other child who may be affected by the birth.' It also deals with some associated matters: making provision that recipients of donated genetic material are nonetheless to be treated in law as parents of the resulting child, and amending the Surrogacy Arrangements Act 1987. Finally it amended the Abortion Act 1967 relating to medical termination of pregnancy. The HFE Act lays down that a majority of members of the HFEA must not be professionally involved in the areas it regulates. No assisted conception treatment or procedures involving gametes or embryos covered by the Act may be performed except under licence granted by the HFEA. In addition to considering applications for licences for treatment, embryo storage or research, the HFEA is required to:

(a)   keep a formal register of information about donors, treatments and children born from those treatments. This is so that offspring born as a result of donated eggs or sperm can find out, if they wish, something about their genetic background;

(b)   produce a Code of Practice which gives guidelines to clinics about the proper conduct of licensed activities;

(c)   publicise its role and provide relevant advice and information to patients and donors and to clinics;

(d)   keep under review information about embryos and any subsequent development of embryos and about the provision of treatment services and activities governed by the HFE Act, and advise the Secretary of State, if he asks it to do so, about those matters.

Contravention of the HFE Act will, upon conviction, constitute an offence and be punishable by imprisonment up to a maximum of ten years, or a fine, or both.

13. We take the view that it is appropriate and necessary that the various practices associated with the relief of infertility should be subject to regulation, and we welcome many aspects of the legislation. We are aware, however, of the continuing debate which surrounds these issues. The HFEA has initiated discussion of particular questions, and such debate is of continuing importance.

14. In our discussions, although we have acknowledged the importance and value of 'natural law', we have also been aware that arguments based on it only too:

> frequently spring from a mentality which prefers to canonise the past and the familiar than to explore the unknown and the future....In this it is profoundly mistaken, for the characteristically human qualities are intelligent control of the environment coupled with respect. In more religious terms, the difference is one between the passive acceptance of God's gifts and finding in them the challenge of active stewardship....[9]

Although it would be wrong to dismiss the natural law tradition too cavalierly, it is obviously necessary to beware of its seductiveness.

15. The arguments about assisted conception matters have inevitably but sadly inherited the dissensions and traditions of the abortion debate.[10] On the one hand, English law has accepted that there are circumstances which allow the therapeutic termination of pregnancy; on the other, there are many Christians who regard the legalisation of abortion as a symptom of and spur to moral decadence. It is not easy to reconcile the extreme views expressed in the abortion controversy, and it has to be accepted that a similar polarisation is manifest in the debate about new reproductive technologies.

Footnotes

1   Board for Social Responsibility: Evidence to the DHSS Inquiry into Human Fertilisation and Embryology (GS Misc 172) (24 February 1983).

2   Board for Social Responsibility: Human Fertilisation and Embryology. The Response of the Board for Social Responsibility to the DHSS Report of the Committee of Inquiry (November 1984).

3   Sacred Congregation for the Doctrine of the Faith: Declaration on Abortion (1974).

4   Department of Health and Social Security: *Report of the Committee of Inquiry into Human Fertilisation and Embryology.* Cmnd 9314 (July 1984). Paragraph 11.9.

5   Ibid. Paragraph 11.17.

6   O'Donovan, Oliver: *Begotten or Made? Human Procreation and Medical Technique.* Oxford University Press (1984).

7   The Catholic Bishops' Joint Committee on Bio-Ethical Issues: *Response to the Warnock Report* (1984).

8   Mahoney, J: *Bioethics and Belief.* Sheed & Ward (1984), pp. 54–5.

9   Mahoney, op. cit. p.16.

10 Council for Science & Society: *Human Procreation, Ethical Aspects of the New Techniques.* Oxford University Press (1984).

1

Developments in assisted conception techniques

16. The inability to have children is recognised to be a source of great distress and unhappiness to many of the couples so affected. Involuntary infertility is thought to affect as many as one in ten couples (although accurate figures on incidence are not available). Infertility affects both sexes and it has many causes. Some forms are amenable to correction by conventional surgical and medical means; others, however, do not respond to such measures. Medical science has attempted to resolve the more persistent forms of infertility by developing a number of assisted conception techniques, thereby enabling couples to have children who would otherwise be denied them.

17. The world's first 'test tube' baby was born in 1978. This event brought the advances of medical science in this field to the attention of the world. A responsible society needs to give careful thought to the new choices represented in these developments and to the moral and social questions implicit in them. If we are to respond to these questions it is essential that we first understand the nature of these developments in assisting conception.

Artificial insemination by husband or donor

18. Not all the techniques used are new. The artificial insemination of the wife by semen from the husband (AIH) or an unrelated donor (formerly AID, now referred to as DI, Donor Insemination) has been used widely and successfully for over 50 years. In the United Kingdom in 1994, there were 1671 babies born by means of DI.

19. AIH has traditionally been used when the husband's infertility is due to the production of too few, or insufficiently motile, sperm. Semen is collected on several occasions, concentrated in the laboratory and then

introduced artificially into the wife at the receptive time of her cycle. The couple are thus aided to have a child they would otherwise be unable to have. Both are the natural parents of the child. It is now used less commonly than previously because of technical developments (Paragraph 35) although these do not change the moral position.

20.   As reproductive techniques have developed, it has become evident that there are several different aspects to parenthood which must be distinguished. There are as yet no formal names for these components. Under normal circumstances, the natural parents are both the genetic and the social parents, and additionally, the woman is the physiological mother. The genetic or biological parents are those who have provided the hereditary material for the child by way of the sperm and ovum. The social parents care for and are legally responsible for the child. The physiological mother carries and nurtures the child prenatally and gives birth to him or her. Some of the new techniques separate these various strands of parenthood so that they are carried out by several different people rather than just the one couple.

21.   If the male partner is unable to produce sufficient sperm for fertilisation or if he is likely to transmit a serious inherited disease, sperm from an unrelated donor can be used to inseminate the woman. This is only done after full discussion with the couple of the implications and possible consequences, and requires the consent of both partners. In this case, both partners are the social parents of the child but only the woman is also the genetic parent. The male partner is unrelated to the child genetically, it is the donor who is the genetic father.

22.   Donors are often medical students, less commonly married men, of known potency. Until 1996, payments could be made for donations. This was limited by direction of the HFE Act to £15 for each donation, plus reasonable expenses. From 1996 payments were phased out and donors now receive only reimbursement for expenses incurred directly as a result of making the donation. The HFEA has stated that a donation should be a gift, freely and voluntarily given. From the Christian point of view, it is clearly inappropriate that donors should sell their gametes for gain. Sperm (and eggs, Paragraph 32) are not commodities to be bought and sold: they are God-given means of making possible the gift of new life. In the past, by convention, each donor provided sperm for only a limited

number of pregnancies, to reduce the chance of later incestuous unions, but this was not mandatory. The HFEA Code of Practice lays down that no more than 10 children may be born from any one donor. The donor remains anonymous to the recipients, but the practitioner will try to match certain physical characteristics of the donor such as major blood groups, eye and hair colour, build and height to those of the male partner. The HFEA is required to keep this information on its register of genetic donors, and can on request disclose it and other non-identifying information to the child when he or she attains the age of 18 years. The donor has no legal or parental rights over or responsibilities to the child. The woman's partner is the legal father of the child, unless he can prove that he did not consent to the treatment.

In vitro fertilisation

23.   In vitro fertilisation (IVF) can overcome female infertility, and may be regarded very broadly as the female equivalent of AIH.

24.   The term 'in vitro fertilisation' is a more accurate description of the method involved than 'test tube baby'. The technique was devised to aid women whose infertility is due to blocked or damaged fallopian tubes (structures which connect the ovaries with the uterus) so that ova (eggs) and sperm are unable to meet at the correct site for fertilisation. Blocked tubes arise because of damage or disease, which in turn may occur because of a previous ectopic pregnancy (the foetus growing elsewhere, not in the uterus), a congenital abnormality or a past infection. The technique normally involves the hormonal stimulation of the ovary and monitoring of the growth of the follicles (the maturing eggs) by ultrasound until they are judged to be ripe, whereupon several ova are removed surgically under sedation. Occasionally natural unstimulated cycles are used. In the laboratory, the ova are mixed with sperm in vitro (in a glass dish) and fertilisation, and the growth of the newly formed embryo through its first few cell divisions, take place in that dish within an incubator. Two to three days after egg collection up to three embryos (see Paragraph 27) are transferred to the woman's uterus through the vagina and cervix. Hormone treatment ensures optimal receptivity, and if all goes well thereafter one or more embryo(s) will implant. They are then nurtured prenatally and deliv-

ered as a normal pregnancy. In 1994, more than 3000 children were born in the United Kingdom by this method.

25.   The parallels with AIH are that both partners are the genetic as well as the social parents. IVF differs, however, in that some risk has been incurred by the woman through the hormone treatment and the invasive procedure necessary to collect the ova. She is also more likely than usual to have a multiple birth which involves some risk to both mother and babies. Further, more embryos are often produced than can be used at one time and a decision has to be made about their fate.

26.   This form of IVF may aid some other types of infertility, such as when the woman has antibodies to the man's semen so that she destroys the sperm placed in her reproductive tract, and when the man has such marked oligospermia that he produces too few sperm even to pool for AIH, or when he produces sperm which have a severe defect of motility. The technique of IVF was pioneered in England, but its use has rapidly spread world-wide and many thousands of children have now been born as a result of it. From the available data the incidence of birth defects in these children seems to be no higher than in children produced by natural means. If this is so, then in this respect the technique can be regarded as incurring no extra risk to the children.

27.   Although some practitioners use only the single egg arising from a regular natural ovulation, far more often hormonal stimulation of the ovary is employed so that several ova ripen simultaneously, and these are harvested and fertilised. (Unfertilised eggs cannot as yet be successfully stored.) Thus, several embryos may be available to be transferred to the woman at any one time; however, the HFEA has set an upper limit of three embryos per treatment cycle. It has been found that the chances of implantation are increased if two or three embryos are transferred together, although it also increases the chance of a multiple pregnancy, which is medically attended by more complications than a singleton preg-nancy, and more than one child is more demanding on the parents. Many couples however, regard a multiple pregnancy as a bonus after years of childlessness. Overall, there are increased risks and costs associated with IVF pregnancies and births compared with those from natural concep-tions, but as with treatment for other conditions, the risks and costs are weighed against the benefits to the patient concerned.

Cryopreservation

28.   The hormonal stimulation of ovulation may result in the production of many eggs and thus, after fertilisation, many embryos over and above the three which may be transferred to a woman at any one time. It is possible for surplus embryos to be frozen and stored in liquid nitrogen at −197°C for several years. These may then be used for the couple on another occasion, either in a later cycle if the first transfer did not yield a pregnancy or, if the first was successful, much later to produce a sibling. The embryos are simply thawed and then transferred to the mother as before, the advantage for the mother being that she does not have to undergo the intensive hormone treatment, monitoring and invasive egg recovery. As yet, no adverse effects of freezing and thawing have been demonstrated, but long-term follow-up studies are necessary. In 1993, there were 450 babies born in the United Kingdom following cryopreservation and in 1994 the number was 401. The HFE Act stipulated that the maximum time for storing embryos should be five years. In practice, this was found to be too short a time period for some couples who wished to space the children in their families produced by this means. In 1996, a new statutory instrument extended the permitted storage period to ten years in most cases. However, parents must specifically consent to the extended storage. In exceptional circumstances, embryos may be stored for more than ten years. There are some embryos in storage whose parents have failed to keep in contact with the clinic and who cannot be traced; these embryos are allowed to perish when their time limit expires. This is an area of concern to some Christians, but not to others.

Spare embryos

29.   Frequently, the situation arises when surplus embryos are no longer required by the parents. The HFE Act allows them to be used for donation to other infertile couples, or for licensed research with the consent of the parents. Research is permitted only up to 14 days of age or to the stage of development of the primitive streak, an observable structure normally formed by day 14 (see Paragraph 90). If they are not used for research or treatment they are allowed to perish and be discarded. No research on embryos is permitted unless its goal and method are approved and licensed by the HFEA.

Related techniques

30.   There is an increasing number of related techniques. Some cases of female infertility such as cervical mucus defects can be treated by GIFT (Gamete Intra-Fallopian Transfer), whereby eggs and sperm are collected as in IVF, but then a maximum of three eggs are mixed with the sperm and immediately transferred to one or both of the woman's fallopian tube(s). Fertilisation then occurs as it normally does, within the woman. Since this is so, GIFT does not at present come under the control of the HFEA unless donor gametes are involved.

Wider applications of IVF

31.   The basic procedures of ovum collection, fertilisation *in vitro* and embryo transfer are available for use in situations other than those already described, for which they were originally devised. There are a number of permutations.

Ovum donation

32.   If the woman is unable to produce ova, or is likely to transmit a seriously disabling inherited condition, or has a severe pelvic disorder which prevents egg recovery, but has a uterus which will support a pregnancy, then an ovum donated by another woman may be fertilised *in vitro* by her partner's sperm, and the resulting embryo replaced in the woman. The man is then the genetic and the social father, but the woman is not the genetic mother, although she is both the social and the physiological mother, having nurtured the child prenatally and delivered it. This is ovum donation. It is the female parallel of DI in the sense that it uses a donated gamete. In 1994, 170 babies were born in the United Kingdom using donor eggs. The demand for this procedure far outstrips the supply of donor eggs. Until 1996, donors could be paid £15 plus reasonable expenses or be offered free treatment or sterilisation. From 1996, payment in money or kind is no longer permitted.

Embryo donation

33.   If both partners are unable to produce gametes, then both the sperm and the ova could be provided by donors, fertilisation brought about *in vitro* and the embryo transplanted into the woman. In this case neither of the partners is the genetic parent, but they would both be the social parents. In this respect the situation is similar to adoption. Embryo donation is sometimes called 'prenatal adoption'. But there is possibly a difference since, in this instance, the social mother also provides the pre-natal nurture and delivers the child. It is thought that this intimate prenatal association produces increasing bonding of the mother to the baby she carries as pregnancy progresses, which is of natural benefit for the subsequent postnatal relationship. However, no actual measure of this benefit has yet been demonstrated. In 1994, 48 babies were born in the United Kingdom from donated embryos.

Surrogate motherhood

34.   If the female partner has a defect of the uterus or the uterus has been removed, or there is some physical handicap or medical condition such as heart or kidney disease which renders pregnancy impossible or dangerous, then her ovum could be fertilised *in vitro* with her partner's sperm and the embryo transferred to the uterus of another (third party) woman for prena-tal development. The usual expectation is that the baby would be handed over to the couple after delivery. This is a contractual arrangement and it is this which is known as surrogacy. The couple would be the genetic parents and the social parents but the female partner would not be the physiolog-ical mother. It is the fact that the woman who actually bears and delivers the child, then severs all relationship and responsibility, which causes con-cern. There are a number of variants of the procedure involving different combinations of donors of the egg and sperm. Some can still be regarded as medically justified because they overcome the problem of infertility or genetic disease. However, they also include others which are way outside these medical reasons. No surrogacy arrangement is enforceable by law. But, to simplify the consequences of a successful surrogacy arrangement, a new legal instrument came into effect in 1995 entitled 'Parental Orders'. This allows, on the birth of a child to a surrogate mother, the transfer of legal responsibility to the commissioning parents from the surrogate mother without the need for full adoption procedures.

Male infertility

35.   In around 40% of infertile couples the problem lies with the male rather than with the female. Again, the causes are many and AIH and DI are two techniques which can be used in such cases. More recent techniques may also involve *in vitro* fertilisation and are increasingly used to help couples where the males produce few active sperm. An example is ICSI (Intra-Cytoplasmic Sperm Injection) where an individual sperm is injected into an egg. Some concerns have been expressed about risks connected with this technique; as with all new techniques, the HFEA is monitoring this process closely.

Other possibilities arising from these new techniques

36.   There are other collateral applications and developments of these techniques which should be considered.

Genetic screening

37.   The genetic screening of embryos produced by IVF is now possible for certain genetic diseases, and in principle, will be possible for all single-gene disorders once the respective genes have been identified and cloned. Diagnosis is performed on the embryos at the eight-cell stage. One cell is removed, its DNA amplified, and the presence or absence of the disease gene in question determined. This can be done in 24 hours, and is harmless to the embryo because at that early stage, all cells have the same potential and the loss of one can readily be made good. Only embryos diagnosed as free from the disease are subsequently transferred to the mother, those shown to be affected by it are allowed to perish. This technique can be used for fertile couples who are known to be carriers of specific genetic diseases. It enables them to have only children free from the disease. Currently, this is usually achieved by the prenatal diagnosis of an established pregnancy by chorion villus sampling at 12 weeks or by amniocentesis in the mid-trimester, with late abortion of affected foetuses. Pre-implantation *in vitro* diagnosis avoids this. As with other advances, it is essential that the HFEA and society in general should keep the ethical implications of advances in genetic screening under careful review.[1]

Gene therapy

38.   Gene therapy is the genetic modification of cells, usually by the introduction of a new gene, but it can also involve the inactivation of an existing gene. Somatic cell gene therapy involves the modification of specific body cells such as bone marrow cells. It often involves inserting the normal counterpart of the disease gene into selected cells from an affected individual. This affects only the individuals concerned, it is not passed on to succeeding generations, and is little different in principle from such therapies as organ transplantation. Germ-line therapy involves genetic manipulation of the reproductive cells. This can be achieved in a number of ways, but crucially, the effects are transmitted to all future generations. Somatic cell gene therapy is presently being developed as a form of treatment for individuals with certain genetic diseases. In principle, this could also be applied to embryos. However the HFE Act prohibits the alteration of the genetic structure of any cell while it forms part of an embryo. Further, and quite separately, in a recent decision on the future of gene therapy, it has been agreed only to pursue somatic cell therapy, and not germ-line therapy for the time being.[2]

Sex selection

39.   The identification of the sex of the embryo is possible by removal of a single cell from an early embryo and testing it with molecular probes. Therapeutically, it aids couples at risk for sex-linked genetic diseases where, most usually, only males are affected. Embryos shown to be female are replaced in the mother, and all male embryos are discarded. Sex selection is permitted for these purposes. However, as research progresses and the individual genes responsible for sex-linked diseases are identified, increasingly a precise diagnosis can be made in each embryo, and unaffected male embryos can be replaced in the mother as well as females. But sex selection may be desired for social reasons, and in 1993, the HFEA initiated public consultation as to whether the use of assisted conception techniques for sex selection was desirable for social, as opposed to medical, reasons. As a result of the responses received, it was decided not to permit this.[3]

Research

40.   There are two routes by which embryos might become available for research. Firstly, they could arise incidentally as spare embryos from infertility treatment programmes, having been produced with the idea of being transferred to the mother, but becoming surplus to requirements. Secondly, they could be created specifically for research purposes, with no prior intention of transfer to the mother.

41.   The HFE Act permits the creation and use of human embryos for research, but research may be performed only under licence granted by the Human Fertilisation and Embryology Authority. The HFEA must be satisfied that the use of human (as opposed to animal) embryos is essential. Licences are granted to specific projects considered individually, rather than to research establishments or individuals. The research must conform to strict criteria and must appear to be necessary or desirable for the purpose of (a) promoting advances in the treatment of infertility; (b) increasing knowledge about the causes of congenital diseases; (c) investigating the causes of miscarriages; (d) developing more effective techniques of contraception; (e) developing methods for detecting the presence of a gene or chromosome abnormalities in embryos before implantation. It is a criminal offence to (a) place a human embryo in an animal; (b) place an animal embryo in a woman; (c) replace the nucleus of a cell of an embryo with a nucleus taken from another embryo or from the cell of another person; or (d) alter the genetic structure of any cell while it forms part of an embryo. In addition, the HFEA will not issue licences for cloning by means of embryo splitting, either for treatment or research. (Cloning is the creation of multiple genetically identical individuals.) The HFE Act also prohibits keeping or using an embryo after the appearance of the primitive streak (14 days after fertilisation). The consent of the parents of the embryos used in research must be obtained, the research project must have the approval of the local hospital ethics committee before a licence application is considered, and the licensing procedure itself involves the refereeing of the application by two independent experts in addition to consideration by the HFEA.

Other ethical dilemmas

42. New developments in this ever-widening field occur at an astonishing pace. Some recent ethical dilemmas not discussed in detail here include the following: should there be an upper age limit for fertility treatment since it is now possible for post-menopausal women to become pregnant? Should ova from women of one ethnic group be used to treat women from other ethnic groups? Should women be permitted to specify a donor egg from an ethnic group other than their own? Should assisted conception be performed for lesbian women? (the HFE Act does not explicitly prohibit this). The HFE Act directs that the Code of Practice guidance concerning the welfare of children born as a result of treatment services should include consideration of a child's need for a father. Nevertheless some, but not all, clinics do treat lesbian couples.

Concluding comment

43. Much of modern medicine consists of manipulating biological processes to remedy a disordered situation. In most spheres this is perfectly acceptable, but the field of reproduction is an exception. This is because there is far more at stake than the individual with the disorder; reproduction involves the creation of another individual who must be considered. However, exactly how much consideration should be given to that other individual and from what moment that consideration should be given are central issues in the current debates on the ethics of these new reproductive technologies. From the earliest times there has been concern for human life before birth. Until now, this has been discussed in the context of the abortion of a recognisable foetus from an established pregnancy. The new reproductive technologies focus the debate far more sharply and extend the discussion right back to the beginning, when the embryo is composed of only one cell and cannot even be seen by the naked eye.

The fear of genetics

44. In Brave New World, Aldous Huxley described a world where men and women were produced for social and industrial needs. Individuals were 'made' for particular jobs by growing and conditioning zygotes of particular constitutions. People were manipulated simply as machines. Looking

back 27 years later (in *Brave New World Revisited*, 1958) he found the night-mare catching up on him:

> The completely organized Society, the scientific caste sys-tem, the abolition of free will by methodical conditioning, the servitude made acceptable by regular doses of chemi-cally induced happiness . . . the much too orderly Brave New World where perfect efficiency left no room for freedom or personal initiatives (is) coming much sooner than I thought they would.

Other latter-day prophets (George Orwell, Desmond Morris, Rattray Taylor, Richard Lewontin) have described exactly the same sort of deter-minism: men and women becoming lost units in a massive web where they can no longer express themselves except by eccentricity or violence.

45.   This sort of determinism is far removed from the Judaeo-Christian tradition where individuals are seen to have dignity and responsibility, and to be capable of personal response to a loving God. It has, however, been apparently strengthened in the particular field of knowledge with which we are concerned in this report. As knowledge of gene action has progressed, we now know that genes act chemically, but this may secondarily affect behaviour (as in Down syndrome), stature (as in achon-droplasia, an inherited form of marked limb shortening) or intelligence (as in phenylketonuria, a metabolic disorder which effectively 'poisons' the brain, resulting in mental retardation). A few years ago, the discovery that a proportion of tall, aggressive male criminals with low intelligence had an extra Y chromosome (that is, instead of the normal XY male sex chromo-some complement, they were XYY), led to claims that they were incapable of modifying their behaviour, and could not be held responsible for their actions. This conclusion cannot be sustained. It is now recognized that some XYY men may be entirely normal in physique and behaviour, but more importantly, an inherited disposition does not absolve from moral responsibility. Notwithstanding, the assumed link between genes and behaviour has given rise to a mechanistic interpretation supported by sci-entific humanists such as Jacques Monod, E. O. Wilson and Richard Dawkins.[4] Their argument is that we are, in effect, the prisoners of our genes. Our behaviour, ability, and personality are, they assume, deter-mined by our genetic composition, and we are only capable of affecting this to a comparatively small extent.

46.   This conclusion does not follow from the facts. Although our genes may limit our individual potential in particular ways, they do not control our actions or restrict our responsibility for them. Genes can be regarded as analogous to the blueprint of a building. They direct the formation and nature of various gene-products (which are simple proteins). These gene-products then interact together and with their surroundings. As the blueprint is clearly not the final building, so the genes do not constitute the individual. Although an individual has to accept the genes he or she possesses, in some cases they can be counteracted to some extent. For example, people who have inherited phenylketonuria can be prevented from developing the irreversible changes to their brains if they are reared on a diet free of the amino acid, phenylalanine. Haemophiliacs can be relieved of their symptoms by treatment with Factor VIII and diabetics with insulin, and so on. In other words, the genes we are born with do not necessarily determine our life and health. Even in the limited chemical sense we are more than the sum of our genes. Since we believe also that we are made in the image of God, and are distinct in this respect from all other animals, it becomes doubly clear that the deterministic pessimism of the *Brave New World* ilk does not apply in the particular field of genetics – or indeed elsewhere.[5]

47.   Genetic determinism is a scientific expression of the common assumption that we are nothing but machines, and hence there is no room for God in our actions and intents. Considering the number of times that this particular heresy has been answered, it is irritatingly persistent. It is important to deal with it here, because if we regard ourselves as nothing but the sum of our genes, we are automatically led to over-value the importance of our genetic composition, and the zygote from which we sprang.

The way forward

48.   In recent years there has been a flood of books and articles describing the medical, social and ethical consequences of the procedures listed in this chapter. We list some background reading in Appendix II. In this chapter we have defined some of the technical terms, but readers are referred to other works for the medical and scientific background of the moral problems described in this document. Our aim is to set these problems in their historical and theological context. We are conscious that new

discoveries require us to look again at the conclusions philosophers and theologians have drawn in the past; our approach has been to examine where appropriate the grounds on which the conclusions were made. In doing this we have sought to be faithful to scripture and to tradition, challenging these only where new information shows that scripture has been misinterpreted or that tradition has been based on false premises. In this way we are seeking to be faithful to the truth. Certainly we have been continually aware of the danger of adapting our ethics to scientific advances, or falling into the trap of devising a morality for therapeutic importunists.

49.   Notwithstanding, we have thought it right to be positive (some will call it iconoclastic) in our approach, believing that the Church has a responsibility to contribute. The IVF pioneer Dr R. G. Edwards pointed out his personal need for help in the 1963 Horizon Lecture:

> We have looked for inspiration to philosophers, theologians, lawyers, for their wisdom gained from centuries of debate about ethics, about human standards, in relation to the implications of new work (on the technology of human reproduction). This search for advice, for leadership, for clarity from the traditional purveyors of moral standards, usually ends in confusion. There is confusion between the great religions of the world . . . It is the same with philosophers . . . . Nor do the lawyers give us much help.

50.   It is for these reasons that strictly scientific developments in embryology and physiology are relevant to the deliberations of moralists and theologians; and also because fundamental questions affecting our understanding of the nature and status of human life, of the relationship of people to the world in which they live, and of the nature of marriage and the family are raised by these developments that we believe it necessary to face the challenge of these techniques from a Christian perspective.

Footnotes

1   Nuffield Council on Bioethics (1993). *Genetic Screening: Ethical Issues*. Report of the Working Party on Genetic Screening.

2   Committee on the Ethics of Gene Therapy (1992). *Report of the Committee on the Ethics of Gene Therapy*. CM 1788 HMSO, London.

3   Human Fertilisation and Embryology Authority (1993). *Sex Selection: Public Consultation Document*. HFEA Press Release (20 July 1993).

4   Monod, J. (1972). *Chance and Necessity*. London: Collins; Wilson, E.O. (1975). *Sociobiology: The New Synthesis*. Cambridge, Mass: Harvard University Press; Wilson, E.O. (1978). *On Human Nature*. Cambridge, Mass: Harvard University Press; Dawkins, R. (1976) *The Selfish Gene*. Oxford University Press.

5   The horrors of genetic manipulation by tyrants can be answered in exactly the same way. We are more easily manipulated by changing our environment than our genes, but even a science-fiction monster who manipulated human genes would have to reckon with the environment(s) that those genes occurred in.

2

Human dominion

51.   When, as Christians, we come to consider questions of the responsible control of human procreation and the possibilities of genetic
experimentation and control, we are faced with the issues of human control over nature in its deepest form. Do the natural processes of the world,
do the purposes of God, permit or encourage us to exercise control in
these areas? And if so, in which direction? These issues are so new and
challenging that it would be unwise to expect all Christians to agree on
answers to them. They must be carefully considered in detail and the various moral issues involved in them unravelled and clearly faced. But, even
before the detailed issues are confronted, it is important to try and
uncover some of the most general and basic attitudes which may prompt
our decisions. One of these is the question of what our view of nature is –
is it a realm whose limits are set unchangeably, or a world in process perhaps towards an as yet unrealised goal? Secondly, what is our view of the
relation of nature and God's purpose – has he set purposes in nature,
which we ought not to frustrate, or are we free, or indeed do we have a
duty, to shape nature towards the realisation of a moral goal? And thirdly,
what is our view of the limits of human responsibility – are we bound to
respect the natural order of things, just as it is, or is nature a morally neu-
tral order upon which we may impose what we perceive to be good
purposes?

The impact of modern science

52.   The background against which these matters have to be discussed
is the profound impact which scientific developments have had on our
thinking, expectations and experience. We are bound to take note of how
vastly things have changed after the remarkable explosion of knowledge
and increasing control of nature since the seventeenth century. The extent
of the control we can exercise over life is immeasurably extended. Our

ability to make radical changes for better or for worse leaves us with the most far-reaching decisions for which we need discernment into the purposes of God in the world. The changes which have been so formative in the development of our culture have made the relation of human beings and nature a problem to us in our time.

53.   We can view these changes in two related ways. First, the revolution of thought as exemplified in the Newtonian understanding which explicitly rejected the whole Aristotelian-based framework erected in the twelfth and thirteenth centuries. Aristotle believed that all things had proper or essential natures and they had final ends or purposes. Each sort of thing had an inner purpose to realise its own proper nature as fully as possible. Science proceeded by trying to discover the true nature of things and purposes in natural processes. From Newton onwards scientific thought progressively abandoned this framework. The natural world, studied by the sciences, was best understood by means of mathematically expressible general laws. It subsequently became clear that a very large amount, if not all, of evolutionary development occurs by random mutation and selection by environment, in accordance with such laws, which need make no mention of purposes. Nature did not appear to come complete and fixed into natural kinds by the hand of the Creator. It is a continuum of development and gradation, still in process of adaptation, and much that happens in it appears to be random and probabilistic in character.

54.   Second, the revolution in human activities which allowed this knowledge to be used to investigate and construct things. Great changes have taken place which have affected human *making*. The revolutions in industrial production and in technological development have led to the development of complex and sophisticated automated procedures for the making of things. People have used natural forces to harness new modes of energy such as electricity and nuclear fission. Natural materials have been transformed into synthetic materials to serve our needs. In these ways more and more artificial layers have been created between human beings and the nature upon which they work.

55.   Another, possibly more fundamental, aspect of dominion concerns the way humans know and perceive the world. The development of technology is dependent upon distinctive ways of knowing which have been perfected by the experimental sciences since the seventeenth century.

Although there has been a vast increase in our knowledge since these developments, this has also involved the loss of certain understandings which an earlier age thought it could possess. For example, the knowledge of a unifying order has been lost in a fragmented pluralism of the different experimental disciplines. As the knowledge of processes has developed so the cohesive unity of knowledge (of natural kinds) has been lost to us.

56.   Thus the development of science and technology has deeply affected the way we perceive the world and the way we believe we may make use of it. We have moved from a world in which experience constantly spoke of the limits of human ability to intervene in the natural order to one in which we wonder whether there are any limits on what we can do with the natural world. In the light of this revolution of knowledge and technical skill which itself arose in response to a new perception of the natural order of the created universe, we are compelled to examine anew the relationship of nature to the divine purpose.

Christian responses

57.   We ought not to be surprised by the fact that Christians react in different ways to these changes. In considering modern developments in the field of human embryology we ourselves have reacted in two contrasting ways. The first is to welcome the changes in thought and experience that have taken place. This is linked with a readiness to accept new knowledge and more accurate ways of understanding the natural order. The creative process continues and involves ever-widening horizons of human knowledge and capability. We are in the midst of a journey whose beginnings lay in creation and whose end is to be realised in the hope given to us in Jesus Christ. The Christian task, therefore, in the face of new demands on human responsibility is a constant search to turn both knowledge and practice to good ends. In terms of the Divine purpose, we must seek it through a developing process which is shaped towards some ultimate good, but not yet achieved goal. If this is so, we cannot simply look for the preservation of human nature as it has been, as though perfection was in the past, and all change must be degeneration. Instead, we need to think how the world should be and how we can either protect its integrity or realise its God-given possibilities so as to advance towards the realisation of God's purpose.

58.   The second reaction is to reflect on what we may have lost in the process of the development of modern scientific knowledge and practice. This suggests we are in danger of losing any serious sense of the boundaries of natural law and of the purposes for which things are created by God. We run the risk of over-estimating human abilities and our place in relation to nature. We fail to consider that God may have set limits in the natural order which we, if we are to remain faithful in our stewardship of the world, should respect and not seek to breach. Essential perspectives for the understanding of our place in the world are liable to be lost sight of in our culture. Surrounded by what we have made, we are in danger of constructing everything as an artefact and forgetting the reciprocal relations between ourselves and the given non-human order. Thus our very creativity falls victim to its own success because it leads to a loss of its essential correspondence to an objective structure of meaning. We are in danger of being reduced to merely describing the process of the changes we are involved in and, thereby, of being cut off from talking about (a) the value and purpose of nature; (b) the distinctiveness of humankind in the created order; and (c) the creative purposes of God in the natural order.

59.   These two contrasting reactions need not be mutually exclusive. They do, however, tend to different evaluations of the ethics involved in the development of modern technology in human embryology. The former attitude is clearly more open to the possibilities in these developments of enhancing human living. The latter is more cautious of their effect upon the way we understand our place in the world. These differing viewpoints result in differing emphases in theological and ethical conclusions and they are themselves the product of contrasting theological and philosophical starting points. Nevertheless they both seek to form judgements about where the moral boundaries for human action on the natural world lie.

60.   In trying to describe the boundaries of Anglican moral discussion there are certain fundamental principles which set the terms of the discussion. These principles are basic to forming a Christian mind on the issues raised by developments in human embryology. If one of the potential temptations in the exercise of human dominion is a temptation to idolatry, which is a sin of thought, it is vital that we establish proper principles for Christian thought in these matters so that we view scientific and technological development in the light of God's purposes and human vocation.

Creation and 'Natural Law'

The universe has been created by God for a purpose, and its basic laws provide some limit or clue to this purpose. It is right therefore that, in some sense, we should posit and seek for 'Natural Law'. We can begin by looking at the structures and possibilities of the natural order in the light of our belief in the Divine purpose for creation. In our scientific/technological culture in which the possibilities of human endeavour appear so extensive, it is important that our mind is shaped by learning to see the world and all of its life under the sovereignty of God, the Father of Jesus.

Order in nature

We accept that there is a structure and order in nature. We should therefore be concerned for the protection of its proper integrity and the realisation of its positive possibilities. We are not free to do as we please. There is a good to be aimed at, and this is the good of nature itself, as destined by God for realisation at the proper time. In thinking about human dominion we have a responsibility to make explicit the structural limits which define it. The simple exercise of power over matter for its own sake has never been what Christians meant by human dominion.

Human responsibility

The human race has a divinely given dominion over and responsibility for the natural order. We are stewards and trustees of what God has made and maintains. We cannot therefore escape our obligation in the light of the divine revelation in Jesus Christ to reflect upon our developing knowledge of the created order and to act accordingly.

Eschatology

Clear thinking about human dominion requires us to attend to eschatology. God's purposes are still, in some sense, unfulfilled and the destiny of the whole world is towards their fulfilment. St Paul speaks in obscure but suggestive language of 'The whole creation therefore groaning in travail' and waiting 'with eager longing for the revealing of the sons of God' (Rom. 8. 22, 19). When we speak of divine providence we do not mean only that God preserves the world as it is; we mean that he preserves it with a view to its ultimate transformation, which is both a liberation from the 'bondage to decay' and the disclosure of new and unforeseen glories. It would be both wrong and foolish to equate this transformation with the march of science and technology. However, Christians may say that the discovery of new possibilities is an aspect of God's providential care and that, whatever our judgement on particular developments, we ought not to fear new things.

The Kingdom of God

Supremely Christians see this transformation as the 'Kingdom of God' which is the sovereign rule of the Creator who will vindicate and confirm his Creator's goodness. Christian eschatology speaks of death and resurrection, not of abandonment and replacement. It is the same world once created that will be redeemed and glorified. It is the good once given that will be vindicated in the end. In our evaluation therefore of what is new we will look not only for the disclosures of new goods for human beings and the world but also for the preservation of those already given. We do not reflect the image of God or the shape of the future by a form of innovation which destroys the good we have received from the past.

Jesus Christ and the Divine purpose

Our understanding of all these matters must focus on Jesus Christ. 'He has made known to us...the mystery of his will, according to his purpose which he sets forth in Christ . . . to unite all things in Him, things in heaven and things on earth' (Eph. 1. 9). There is so much to be gained by studying his teaching, his miracles, his person as described in the New Testament, his authority and his action on and in the world, and especially his death and resurrection. In particular we learn from him of the worth and dignity of human life, of the depth of possibilities for human relationships and of interdependent social life as represented for example in the notion of the church as the 'body of Christ'.

61.   These six principles provide the boundaries and, indeed, the avenue for proper Christian reflection and judgement on the issues facing us in the challenge of the new technologies in human fertilisation and embryology.

62.   Another area of divergence in our understanding of the natural world is more directly theological. It is possible to take different views of the finality of the forms in the created structures of the world as given to

us. Do we celebrate the completion of creation on the seventh day as an accomplished reality, or as a hope yet to be fulfilled? Clearly there is something yet to be fulfilled at the end of history – and not only for socio-political structures (for which theology has usually not made claims of permanence) but for natural structures too. We hope for a new creation, and not only for a restoration and recovery of the creation which sin has damaged. Without such an openness to God's future work there can be no fidelity to the eschatological dimension of the Christian faith. Yet there are different ways of understanding how this hope belongs together with our faith in God as Creator of heaven and earth. Some Christians wish to say that the creative work of God, too, is open-ended and unfinished, as his work in history is unfinished; that the coming Kingdom is precisely the perfecting of the work of creation which is still in process. Others contend for a more 'dialectical' relation between creation and history: openness to the future, they argue, does not imply a creation that is unfinished; the world may have a destiny that is still incomplete without the implication that its forms and structures are still provisional. Such a view suggests an emphasis on the goodness of the created structures as given, and a confidence that thought can disentangle (at least in principle) such permanent goods of creation from the transitory and ambiguous structures thrown up, under divine providence, in the course of history.

63.   We are not agreed as to whether it is possible to see a number of these techniques held within the boundaries of these principles or whether we should be more cautious and fear lest they are examples of human dominion stretching beyond the healthy boundaries of the divine order.

64.   The fact that human persons are body and not merely spirit means that they too can be subject to technical manipulation. The fact that they are spirit, and not merely body, means that there are boundaries to that manipulation. There are moral limits to any human action which restrain us from intending evil and require us to be prudent in what we plan. As we have already argued, there are further moral limits, imposed by God's purposes for nature and for ourselves, on our dominion over nature. We must now consider a further specific area of moral debate, namely the limits to human action on human life.

65.   Both in the New Testament and in patristic moral thought, limits are set down for what we may do with and to our own bodies. Whether the concern is for sexual purity, the distinction between true and false asceti-

cism, or a prohibition on suicide, there is common agreement that we may not treat our bodies as instruments for whatever purposes we choose. They have their own value which means that we are to use them properly and care for them in the service of God. 'The body', says St Paul, 'is not meant for immorality but for the Lord, and the Lord for the body' (1 Cor. 6. 13).

66.   False asceticism improperly portrays bodily life as alienation from our true selves – an imprisonment or humiliation of the spirit. The patristic age understood such false asceticism as self-hatred. The true ascetic aims at the perfect harmony of body and spirit, in which spiritual control of the body is exercised with respect and appreciation. Suicide, as the extreme case of contempt for the body, refuses God his proper claim upon us precisely as living embodied beings. The value placed upon the body is due therefore to the fact that this form of organic life is *human* life – the existence in the body of the human spirit. The human being, as embodied spirit, is called to fellowship with the Holy Spirit (1 Cor. 6. 19). Thus, for Christians, the dignity of the individual involves affirming the dignity of the body. The claim God makes upon the worship of each person he makes upon their bodily existence also.

67.   We turn from this to consider the subject of the often quoted warning that personal dominion over ourselves threatens to become the dominion of some people over other people. The covenant we make one with another, our equality before God and within the community of fellowship, may be threatened if we view one another only as a body which may be used for whatever good purpose we choose. The existence of codes of ethics (such as the Hippocratic Oath and the Helsinki Declaration) governing scientific experiments on human subjects is clear acknowledgement of this. Indeed we can learn from the limits imposed by these codes.

68.   Firstly, there is the requirement of the subject's *free and informed consent* to the experiment. Thus, whatever the risks, the enterprise becomes a partnership between the experimenter and the subject. This guards experimentation from lapsing into tyranny, for although one is experimenting on the body of the other that action is supported by the wills of both people.

69.   Secondly, the full force of these codes is brought to our attention by a further requirement. This is that, if in the course of the experiment the subject is threatened with actual physical harm, the experiment must

cease, in spite of the consent given. In other words I may agree with my experimenter in taking substantial physical risks for the sake of scientific knowledge. My agreement, however, cannot make it right for the experimenter to inflict actual physical harm on me – irrespective of whatever good may ensue. Experimentation therefore still lives inside the terms of the traditional Christian conception that, while we live, our bodies are not simply available for us to dispose of in any way we choose. 'You are not your own; you are bought with a price' (1 Cor. 6. 20).

70.   When we consider experiments on embryos we are into the difficult area of research on human subjects in which the requirement of informed consent cannot be satisfied in its straightforward sense. This is true in a similar manner for very young children. In this case there are different understandings of what consent means. It is possible to take a maximal view and to insist that where the partnership of experimenter and subject cannot be established by the direct giving of consent, the implications of tyranny cannot be removed from any research involving risk of harm. This would appear to prohibit research in these instances. A minimal view, however, would suggest that the partnership may be presumed where the will has not been forced. Thus it is possible to consider consent 'by proxy' which would be given by those who have parental responsibility. It takes the form of a simple agreement that the risks are no more than it would be reasonable to assume another human being to be willing to bear. Such agreement, of course, still has the second requirement for experimental practice that no actual harm will be knowingly inflicted or allowed.

71.   We have come to the threshold of the question of experiments on embryos. It has been reached in the exploration of the terms of human dominion over nature. One provisional comment can be made as we stand on this threshold. It is clear that experiments on embryos would be difficult to justify under these general principles on consent, because of the qualification concerning actual harm, and on either the maximal or minimal (proxy) notions of the meaning of consent. If, therefore, such experiments are to be justified this can only be done by an idea of the ontological status of the embryo, placing it outside the terms which govern our treatment of living human bodies. We cannot therefore proceed with this debate without considering the ontological question of the status of the embryo.

3

The status of the human embryo

72.   In this chapter we set out the key features of the development of the Christian tradition, the facts concerning the development of the early human embryo and what these things mean for the status of the human embryo. The Christian tradition sought to answer moral questions in the light of what was then known about early embryonic life. It is because that tradition was formed before contemporary advances in knowledge about the development of the embryo that we are required to examine again what we believe about the nature and status of the early human embryo.

The Christian tradition

73.   Before entering into a brief description of the Christian tradition, it is important to note one preliminary point. This concerns the varying uses of the concept of the 'soul' in the tradition. In the Old Testament the Hebrew term *nephesh* which is often translated 'soul' usually denotes a person as a *living* being. Indeed the term means breath or life. The body is not seen in the Old Testament as a covering to clothe the soul but as the indispensable and necessary expression of the principle of life. The New Testament continues in this tradition. The 'soul' does not denote a part of a human person but rather the person in his or her character as a living being. It is God who breathed life into Adam and so he became a living soul (I Cor. 15. 45). The New Testament develops this tradition in the light of the person and work of Christ. Paul speaks of the earthly body being transformed into a spiritual body in the resurrection of the body. Christ's resurrection pointed to humanity's true destiny in the experience of eternal life and in the hope of the resurrection of the body. The human person as made by God as a living being had an eternal destiny in Christ crucified and risen. In the early Fathers we begin to see the influence of Greek, and particularly Platonic, thought on the understanding of the soul. Here the notion of the 'soul' as a separate entity created by God, having a form of

its own, began to develop. A human person is a joining of the soul to the body. The soul is eternal and the seat of the knowledge of good and evil and of God. The moment when body and soul are joined is the moment when we have a human person. At death the soul leaves the mortal body and awaits its ultimate destiny in its clothing in the resurrection body.

74.   Medieval theology was much more influenced by Aristotelian concepts of the soul. In particular Thomas Aquinas combined the Augustinian tradition with Aristotelian concepts. In humankind the two great realms of 'form' and 'matter' find their supreme unity. Aquinas rejected Platonic dualism. He was influenced by the Aristotelian notion that the soul can have no life apart from the body. The most developed form of the soul is the rational soul. Together body and soul constitute the unity of the human person. In our use of the term we speak of the human person as made for fellowship with God and for relationships with other persons.

75.   The main question which provoked the Church to consider the status of the embryo concerned abortion. What was to be the Christian response to the practice of abortion? What was permissible for Christians? The comments of the early Fathers are unanimous in their opposition to abortion. Along with condemning murder, fornication, magic and medicine, abortion is condemned in the *Didache*, 'You shall not slay the child by abortions' (*phthora*); 'You shall not kill what is generated...' (*Didache* 2. 2.) The Epistle of Barnabas repeated these condemnations. Clement of Alexandria said that Christians ought not to try to hide their fornication by abortion. That is to take away 'human nature, which is generated in the providence of God' (*Pedagogus* 2. 20. 96:1). Tertullian said, 'It is not lawful to destroy what is conceived in the womb while the blood is still being formed into a man' (*Apologeticum* 1.15). Both the Council of Elvira in 305 and Ancyra in 314 condemned abortion, although they differed on the penalties to be imposed on Christians guilty of this sin.

The formed and unformed foetus

76.   The Septuagint translation of Ex. 21. 22 introduced a distinction into Christian understanding between the 'unformed' foetus and the 'formed' foetus.[1] The Greek text says that life is to be given for life if the embryo is 'formed'. Both Jerome and Augustine explained the tradition that the act was not to be taken to be homicide if the foetus was

'unformed', 'for there cannot yet be said to be a live soul in a body which lacks sensation when it is not formed in flesh and so not yet endowed with sense' (Augustine on the Latin text of Ex. 21. 22). Whilst both Jerome and Augustine remained agnostic about when the soul entered the body they were not prepared to affirm with confidence that this had taken place whilst the foetus was 'unformed'. They did not, however, use the distinction to justify abortion. They were opposed to both contraception and abortion. Nevertheless, only the abortion of a formed foetus could be described as homicide. The question was not whether abortion of an unformed foetus was sin but what sort of sin this represented.

77.   Notwithstanding, the distinction between the formed and unformed foetus was an important one for the development of the Christian tradition. Jerome and Augustine became key texts for the development of medieval canon law in the Western Church. The discussion continued and affirmed that abortion became homicide when the foetus was 'vivified' or 'ensouled'. The decretals of Gregory IX, however, went further and stated that any act which prevented generation and conception was to be treated 'as homicide'. Whilst speculative thought maintained the original distinction and held that abortion before vivification was not homicide, the rules of the Church treated the act as though it were.

78.   Thomas Aquinas maintained the tradition of distinguishing between a formed and unformed foetus and held, in line with Aristotle, that the foetus was vivified at 40 days for a male child and 90 days for a female child.[2] To that time it was 'unformed' and whilst abortion was wrong it could not be taken to be homicide until vivification. Aquinas did not directly rule on the question of whether it was right to abort to save the life of the mother. He did, however, maintain that to kill someone in defence of one's own life was not homicide. Later some of the casuists accepted that therapeutic abortion for the sake of the life of the mother could be accepted whilst the foetus remained unformed. Tomas Sanchez (1530–1610) maintained such a position. St Alfonso de Liguori rejected Sanchez' acceptance of intentional killing of the unformed foetus. The more common opinion, he said, only allowed for abortion as the unintended result of, for example, the mother taking drugs to preserve her life.

79.   The Thomist opinion following Aristotle that the rational soul was not instilled in the body until 40 days did not go wholly unchallenged.

Thomas Fienus in 1620 disputed this view maintaining that the soul was 'infused in the first moment of conception'. This idea had little immediate impact although developments in science were leading to the progressive abandonment of Aristotelian concepts of embryology. However, Papal legislation progressively moved to an almost absolute prohibition of abortion. In 1869 Pius IX dropped the reference to the 'ensouled foetus' in the grounds for excommunication for abortion, thus effectively including all abortions without distinction.

80.   A number of things are clear in this discussion. First, there was universal condemnation of abortion in the early Church. Second, the Septuagint translation of Ex. 21. 22 led to the development of a distinction in considering the embryo between the unformed and formed foetus. Third, the influence of Aristotelian embryology and philosophy led to widespread acceptance of the Thomist solution for 400 or more years which maintained that the rational soul was infused at 40 days which is the time of vivification.

81.   During this period abortion of the unformed foetus was condemned but was not considered to be homicide. This led to discussion as to the possibility of abortion of the unformed foetus in protection of the life of the mother. Throughout, the Christian Fathers sought to apply fundamental Christian convictions about the creation of human life by God to the contemporary understanding of embryology. There were therefore three periods as seen in the tradition: the period up to conception which opened the question of the legitimacy of contraception; the period after conception up to vivification which opened the question of whether there were any circumstances which might justify abortion; and finally, the time after vivification which led to the question of the penalty for homicide in the case of abortion. The questions facing us today require a fresh examination of this tradition by the Church.

The development of the early embryo

82.   Biological life, as such, does not begin at fertilisation. It is a continuum from generation to generation; the egg and the sperm are just as much living as the cells from which they are derived in the gonads and the embryo which together they will produce.

83.   Genetically, the basis for the uniqueness of each embryo is laid down in the cell division called meiosis in the ovaries and testes of the respective parents, when the sperm and the ova are formed. This special cell division determines which particular versions of all the genes will be carried by each gamete. Thus every sperm and ovum is genetically unique whether or not it is involved in fertilisation. A zygote is the result of adding together two unique entities. However, the meeting of a particular sperm and a particular egg is completely unpredictable; it is an apparently chance or random event.

84.   Fertilisation is a process which takes approximately 24 hours to complete, and precedes the beginning of cell division in the zygote produced. Development proceeds continuously throughout gestation and indeed childhood, the brain, for example, continuing to develop for several years after birth. Development involves the gradual appearance of tissues and organs. The situation is not that, for example, one day there is no heart and the next day a heart is present; rather it is that this organ progressively forms and develops. As it does so it acquires occasional contractile movements which gradually become stronger and more frequent and, imperceptibly, a stage is reached where there is a four-chambered structure which 'beats' regularly to circulate the blood.

85.   Although development is a continuous process with an identifiable beginning, it is far from being a simple unfolding of latent potential. Embryology involves a procession of threshold events in which the fate of different parts are qualitatively changed, for example, in the formation of nerve cells from their precursor cells, which would become skin if left to themselves; in the establishment of a nerve net which can function once it achieves a certain complexity; in the production of a hand or foot with five digits from a simple mass of cells; and so on. Thus there are points of qualitative change in the development of the embryo; and some of these may be of great ethical relevance. However, none of these changes involves an abrupt demarcation point between an unformed and formed state; they are all part of a continuum of development.

86.   Normal embryological development does not proceed only by the expression of the intrinsic or genetic factors possessed by the embryo however, but by an interaction of these with extrinsic factors provided by the immediate external environment. Excess or unusual environmental

factors can alter the course of embryological development and may completely inhibit it or produce abnormalities in the embryo. Thus although the actual combination of genes which arises at fertilisation may be said to be unique, fertilisation is necessary but not sufficient to determine the embryo so produced.

87.   Further, although the genetical composition of an embryo is largely fixed when the zygote is formed, it is not immutable. For example, some individuals with Down syndrome possess a mixture of both abnormal and normal cells; although the early embryo contained all abnormal cells which have an extra chromosome, there is a tendency for the extra chromosome to be lost, resulting in a proportion of normal cells. Again, many (perhaps all) cancers arise from a genetic change (mutation) in a cell; a cancer is therefore novel and genetically unique.

88.   Not all conceptions follow the normal pattern of development and culminate in the birth of a baby. Indeed, as many as three-quarters of the eggs which are fertilised are lost, most of them before they implant in their mother's womb about a week after conception. Although it has been known for centuries that some embryos miscarry spontaneously, the magnitude of very early embryonic loss has only recently been recognised.

89.   Moreover, at least half of the fertilised eggs which miscarry are abnormal. Some are so abnormal that development cannot proceed beyond more than a few cells, others develop into embryos with gross major aberrations, while others still proliferate for several weeks but never acquire human form.

90.   Another alteration in the course of normal development occurs in the formation of identical twins. These have an incidence of around 1 in 250 births. At any point from the two-cell stage to the formation of the primitive streak at around 14 days after conception when there are perhaps several thousand cells, the embryo may split into two. These two distinct embryos then develop separately. The primitive streak appears as a heaping up of cells at one end of the midline of the upper side of the embryo. It marks the establishment of bilateral symmetry in the previous assembly of cells, after which twinning can no longer take place. Sometimes, the splitting process is incomplete and then conjoined ('Siamese') twins result. Very rarely, dizygotic twin embryos (non-identical) in the same womb may fuse. If this happens early enough in development,

a single normal birth may result, even though it results from two separate fertilisations.

Different interpretations of the status of the early embryo

91.   It is not surprising that there is more than one way of interpreting the significance of these facts of early human development for our moral attitudes to the unborn. For convenience we may distinguish two broad patterns of interpretation, both of them susceptible to various emphases and nuances, which have emerged in Christian discussion since the coming of widespread abortion made the status of the conceptus a matter of practical controversy.

92.   The first takes its point of reference in *the continuity of the individual subject*. Through and out of the process of prenatal development there emerges an individual, one human being, whose history it constitutes. Consider the contrast between a newborn baby and the individual, 80 years later, who has grown out of that baby; nevertheless we say that the two are the same person. Their identity is not simply a matter of material continuity (which holds, of course, only at the level of organisation, for the actual molecules are not the same), nor of a continuous memory (which does not stretch back to earliest infancy, and may incidentally have been disrupted by psychological trauma). The two are called the same, on the basis of discerning, behind every presentation of the individual human phenomenon, a subject, a 'someone' whom we call by a name, who is the bearer of a particular life history. In Christian faith this insight is expressed in terms of the vocation of every individual by God, and the final judgement of each life history, which gives it a meaning, for good or ill, in the eyes of the Almighty. Starting from the conviction that human beings are subjects, must we not, the first school of thought asks, press back our perception of the continuous subject as far as we can see objective grounds for doing so? We need not be too staggered, we are told, by the major changes and transformations of prenatal life, when no less astonishing changes affect us after birth, without shaking our belief in the continuity of the human subject. This approach, then, traces the individual story back as far as fertilisation, where the sheer contingency of *that* meeting of *those* gametes, one possible meeting out of millions, seems to constitute a wall of arbitrariness behind which the story of the individual cannot be taken any further.

93.   The second interpretation argues that there are attributes which must be possessed by a developing embryo before it can be called a person. Respect is due to an embryo at all stages, but protection of life in the sense that a postnatal child would have it, is afforded only after some particular threshold during pregnancy. This has been variously identified with animation, quickening, sentience or viability. The Warnock Inquiry recommended that protection should be afforded at the time of the formation of the primitive streak since 'this marks the beginning of individual development', and the Board for Social Responsibility in its response to the Inquiry agreed with this position. However, other points of embryonic development can be argued to be crucially significant. For example, the establishment of a functioning nerve net at around 40 days after conception can be regarded as a necessary criterion for the beginning of personal life, paralleling the common acceptance of brain death (as distinct from, say, heart failure) as the mark of the end of physical life.

94.   This second approach is based on the special dignity which is displayed by human nature. To be a human is not merely to participate in one of a multitude of forms of biological life, but it is to be the subject of powers of mind and soul which set humankind apart from other forms of life. At the root of these powers is the phenomenon of consciousness, and it is as *the subject of consciousness*, the proponents of this view maintain, that we value the human being most fundamentally. It is important not to suggest that human beings must exercise some specific degree of intelligence or emotional maturity before they can properly be regarded as human persons. Yet, if we are to draw a morally relevant distinction between humans and other animals, we seem compelled to define the human in terms of a sort of nature able to exercise rational, moral and personal capacities. We need to assert that all members of this species possess such a nature, even where, through some impediment, it cannot be properly exercised in many particular cases. The nature in question, on this view, is traditionally described as that of a 'rational and sensitive soul'. There must be a point at which it may be said that there exists a subject capable in principle and in normal cases of exercising some rational or moral capacities. Adopting the principle that one should err on the side of caution, one may seek to locate the earliest roots of rational, moral and religious activity. One may then look to the first moments of the conscious experience which go to constitute the basis of later rational thought. It is for this reason that con-

sciousness assumes moral importance – not that it is in itself of supreme importance, for animals are also conscious; but that the human subject of the first conscious state is continuous with, and of the same kind as, the subject of a fully developed rational consciousness. Consciousness provides the foundation for those other powers which humans would all exercise if they were not impeded from doing so. In this sense, the human subject, as possessed of unique moral worth, may be properly conceived as the subject of a human form of consciousness. Such a consciousness, at least in its human form, is causally dependent upon certain physical states, and in particular upon certain structures of the central nervous system and the brain stem. The human subject of consciousness, then, cannot come to exist before the development of a body of a certain degree of complexity. It seems plausible to conclude, argue those who adopt this approach, that the human subject – in the strong sense of 'human' in which we recognise humanity as making a special moral claim upon us – cannot take form in an embryonic body which has not yet reached the appropriate stage of differentiation and development.

95.   The tension which can develop between these two approaches when they are confronted with practical questions about the early embryo is well known. We cannot pretend to resolve it, but only to give as clear an account of it as we can, and to point to the underlying theological and philosophical issues. We have come (not without difficulty) to recognise in both these approaches the possibility of a scientifically judicious and theologically responsible set of convictions. But in the heat of public disagreement they may both be badly represented – not least by their opponents! We will attempt a comparison between them which will show up not only where they differ, but what they have in common.

96.   In the first place both approaches attend to the scientific evidence carefully, and attempt to interpret it. That their interpretations are focused upon different features of the evidence should cause no surprise. Science, as such, can only report what happens; it cannot interpret it. It cannot tell us whether the genetic structures of individuality are *more important* to our understanding of what it is to be human than (say) the complexity of the nervous system, or *vice versa*. A decision between the approaches can only be made on theological or philosophical grounds. Yet in deciding that this or that is the crucial feature of the scientific story, advocates of both positions have to resist the temptation either to exaggerate the extent of what

science can say, or to overlook parts of it. The continuity-of-subject tradition, for example, lays great stress on *genetic* evidence for the decisive importance of conception. The significance of this evidence can be, and has been, overstated. For example, it is not true that every human being has a unique genetic code (as the phenomena of twinning and embryo fusion make clear), nor that every human entity which has a unique genetic code is a human being for all the following are genetically unique: every sperm and ovum (Paragraph 83), many tumours and hydatidiform moles which are products of conception formed when two sperm fuse with an egg cytoplasm, having placental but never embryonic development. Nevertheless, when these qualifications have been allowed, genetics has still shown up in a striking light the enormous significance for human individuality of that decisive meeting of sperm and ovum. It has given scientific definition to our intuition that though we are *descended* from our grandparents we are not simply an *extension* of our grandparents – and it has located the genesis of that new thing which is ourselves at a particular point in the long process by which life is handed on. Something similar can be said about the importance attached to the evidence of neurology by the subject-of-consciousness tradition. It is possible to lay claim to more knowledge about the correlation of consciousness and the organisation of the nervous system than can actually be had. Science is far from having proved that human beings are brains encased in flesh; and popular allusions to the conception of 'brain death' – which is really a technique for the *observation* of death – do not lend this idea any additional cogency. Nevertheless, it cannot be denied that the question of physical organisation must be on the agenda whenever we discuss what makes humanity distinctively human. The evidence that brain activity does not occur until some 40 days after conception, does help us to mark an important threshold in foetal development – one which many regard as morally decisive.

97.   In the second place, both approaches have an exegetical concern at heart, and are committed, as *theological* opinions, to achieving a Biblical understanding of humanity and applying it to contemporary questions. Again, the elements they think of most importance in the Biblical conception of humanity differ. Those who think primarily in terms of the human being as a subject of consciousness are concerned especially with the notion that people are made 'in the image of God' (Gen. 1. 26, cf. Jas. 3. 9).[3]

The other school of thought characteristically refers to those texts which speak of individual existence as rooted in the calling of God which ante-dates birth. Texts of special relevance are Luke 1. 41–44 which speaks of John stirring in the womb of Elizabeth when she met Mary the mother of Our Lord; and Luke 1. 34–35 where the angel tells Mary that the Holy Spirit will overshadow her and she will conceive Jesus, Son of the Most High. It has been held that these texts imply an individual human existence well before birth and that the Incarnation sanctifies human life even in the womb.

98.   It is only fair to note, however, that such Biblical references some-times refer to a time even before conception – Jeremiah 1. 4, 'before I formed you in the womb I knew you'. This seems to speak of God's pre-destining will before Jeremiah had even been conceived rather than individual life in the womb. Moreover, where reference is made to embry-onic life nothing is said that could help us to decide whether the very earliest embryos (before six weeks, say) are to be counted as actual human persons. Our Lord was formed of genetic material taken from the body of Mary; but at what stage that material truly becomes an element in the per-son of the Incarnate Word we are not told. Thus the relevant Biblical texts do not clearly force us to adopt one of the two approaches we have out-lined to the exclusion of the other.

99.   Again, both approaches have a proper claim to continuity with elements of Christian tradition. The responsible use of tradition in a discussion like this one is complicated by the inadequacy of the embryology with which earlier generations of Christian thinkers had to work. Nevertheless, we may observe that Christian thinkers of the past believed both in a decisive moment of beginning, given by a new creative act of God himself, and in the possibility, at least, that such a moment belonged not at the very start of the embryo's physical development but some way into it. This latter view – the so-called point of 'animation' – began to fall from favour with the growth of early scientific embryology in the seventeenth century; but it can certainly be claimed that the more complex scientific knowledge of our own time has permitted us to find it illuminating once again. On the other hand, it must also be noticed that the practical pro-tection of the early embryo, justified, if by nothing else, by the speculative uncertainty surrounding the moment of animation, has been more or less complete and consistent in Christian history.

100.   There is an understandable fear that if we allow experimentation on very early embryos fertilised *in vitro* and not implanted in the womb, we may be at the beginning of a 'slippery slope' towards artificially creating embryos for experimentation at much later stages of development. This is something rightly to be feared since all the writers of this report at least strongly agree that experimentation on human subjects, other than to promote their own well-being and with their consent, is morally abhorrent. The 'slippery slope' argument is that if we permit experimentation on 13 day-old embryos it will be harder to resist calls to experiment on 15 day-old embryos and people will find it easier to press for allowing even later experimentation. The answer to the argument is to point out that we all have to draw a line somewhere, whether it is at conception or later. It may be the case that some people will always seek to push beyond that line; but it is not true that the erosion of the line is inevitable. On the contrary, as long as you are clear that a line must be drawn there is no reason why you should not hold to it absolutely. The 'slippery slope' is a real danger only if there is no convincing reason for drawing a line at a particular place. Proponents of both main approaches under discussion, however, have strongly persuasive reasons to support their views. They therefore have equally strong defences against sliding down a 'slippery slope'. It is not the case that those who would ban all experimentation are in a stronger position in this regard than those who would permit it in clearly defined circumstances, with stringent safeguards, and only for extremely important and otherwise unobtainable ends. Both are agreed that the human subject should be given a very high degree of practical protection. The argument is about when the properly human subject may be said to exist.

101.   The root of the divergence, as we have seen, lies in the different ways in which the two schools of thought have framed the question about the human subject, the one concentrating upon its individual continuity, the other on its generic dignity as the subject of consciousness. These two contrasting questions have led in different philosophical directions. A traditional way of characterising this difference would be to contrast their views about the relation of body and soul: on the one hand a stronger emphasis on the transcendence of the soul over the body, on the other a stronger emphasis on the unity of soul and body. But it may also be seen in the different overtones which the word 'person' acquires in the discus-

sions of each school. To each it implies the underlying subject of human attributes; but the one lays stress on the *hiddenness of the subject* which underlies the attributes, which affords substantial continuity through radical change and development, while the other lays stress on the *presence of at least some of the attributes* (rationality, self-awareness, feeling etc.) by which the subject comes to be designated as human. We can observe, without claiming too tight a correlation, certain philosophical compatibilities, which often emerge to view in the characterisations the two schools give of each other in their polemical exchanges. When, for example, the second approach is accused of 'Cartesian dualism' by its opponents, something of truth is being said: not that it is tied to any detailed adherence to the doctrines of Descartes, but that it has a general affinity with the philosophical tradition, which derives its interpretation of the humane from the interior self-knowledge by which human beings can transcend the world of observable objects. The corresponding charge against the first approach, that of an 'Aristotelian biologism', though similarly imprecise, also identifies its philosophical ambit correctly: it looks to observable appearances, to the observed structures, rather than to the interior life which is hidden from us, to judge when another human being first makes a call upon our attention.

102. Serious as this divergence is, and difficult to mediate without resolving a range of major philosophical and theological issues, we may observe that the two schools of thought agree on something which may be of more importance still. They both acknowledge that the human status of the unborn child is something which must be discerned, quite apart from our wishes or our decisions, as a reality which simply commands our recognition as of right. However difficult it may be to decide whether the early embryo is, or is not, a human being, in the most important sense of the term, the question to be resolved is still about whether something is or is not the case, and not some other kind of question. Some of our contemporaries have hoped to avoid the question of the embryo's status altogether, and have thought it possible to move directly to a purely deliberative question: how are we to *act* towards the early embryo? The implication of this manoeuvre would seem to be that human status is not so much discerned as conferred; that social practice is sufficient of itself to validate or invalidate the claims of any pretender to humanity. The authors of this report, though by no means of a common mind as between

the two Christian approaches which we have tried to describe, are agreed in finding this solution unsatisfactory.

Footnotes

1   It is interesting to note the Jewish interpretation of this text. An example of this can be found in the submission made by the former Chief Rabbi, Lord Jacobovits, to the Warnock Committee: 'Man's creation "in the image of God" (Gen. 1. 27) confers infinite value on every innocent human life and renders its destruction into a capital offence (9. 6). While this absolute inviolability – whereby no life may ever be deliberately sacrificed even to save another or any number of others – sets in only at birth (Ex. 21. 12, 22–23, and Jewish commentaries), the unborn child, too, enjoys a very sacred title to life, in different stages from the moment of conception, to be set aside only in exceptional circumstances, such as a serious hazard to the mother.'

2   *Summa Theol.* Qu 118, 2 & 2.

3   There have been various ways in which this phrase has been construed in the history of Christian thought. With the ancient suggestion that it relates to upright stature of humans there is little sympathy among moderns; but other traditional interpretations, suggesting that it has to do with the capacity for relationship with God, with the exercise of dominion over creation, or with the possession of reason and conscience, are often taken up in modern thought, and may perhaps be regarded as complementary rather than mutually exclusive.

4

Marriage and the family

103.   We must begin by setting out what we are and are not doing in this chapter. We are not giving a comprehensive account of the Christian understanding of marriage and of the family. We have a much more limited aim; to consider the Christian understanding of the nature and place of procreation in marriage and the possible meaning of this for the moral acceptability of the use of new technologies aimed at overcoming the problems of childlessness. There are many other aspects of marriage which have been and doubtless will continue to be considered by the Church which are beyond our terms of reference.

104.   It has been traditional in the Western Church to refer to three 'ends' or 'goods' of marriage. St Augustine, with whom the tradition seems to have originated, used to speak of the three as 'offspring, fidelity and sacrament'. The Book of Common Prayer, which has made the tradition familiar to Anglicans, lists them as 'the procreation of children...a remedy against sin...(and) the mutual society, help and comfort which the one ought to have of the other'. The union of two people in the completeness of marriage involving sexual, social, emotional and relational aspects, is seen as promoting three central goods on human life: namely, the transmission of life in the human community, a disciplined structure of living in which the individual may grow to moral maturity, and a strong and enduring relationship between them. In short we may speak of the 'procreational', 'moral' and 'relational' goods of marriage.[1]

105.   This tradition clearly takes a sympathetic view of attempts to relieve childlessness. Such attempts do, after all, assist marriage to fulfil one of its natural ends. There is a longstanding Christian concern that marriage, wherever possible, should lead to parenthood. Childless couples, though their marriage is perfectly valid and is often rich in other virtues, have been disappointed of a good which is proper to them. First, we can see how this tradition will foster a concern that the relief of childlessness should be

undertaken only within marriage and as a service to marriage. 'The procreation of children' is meant in a broad sense: 'bringing them up in accordance with God's will, to his praise and glory' (ASB). The transmission of life in the human community ought not to be viewed in a narrowly biological sense. There is a social aspect, adequate or inadequate, passed on with life itself, and this is of crucial importance to the growth and development of the child. No service is done to procreation if it is taken out of the context of family life in which the Creator wills young human beings to flourish. There is a third implication concerned with this tradition. This is concerned with *holding together* the procreational and relational 'goods' of marriage. This requires some careful examination because it has a profound implication for different ways of resolving childlessness.

106.   We need first to explain what we mean by the use of the interchangeable terms 'end' and 'good'. Here we are using the idea of an 'end' as a purpose rather than a conclusion. The term 'purpose' may be used in two ways or may mean two different things. It may be a goal which we decide upon. This is something we fix upon by the exercise of our own freedom of choice. Second a purpose may be seen as a 'good' which is part of the order of things and something we discern by our reason and accept as part of the given nature of the way things are meant to be. Christians think of these 'goods' as the Creator's purposes for what he has made. It is in this second sense of purpose that we talk of the three 'goods' of marriage. When we enter into marriage we enter an institution given to us by God with these three good ends as part of its nature and meaning. Christians have traditionally believed that these goods should be held together.

107.   When it is said that the procreational and relational goods of marriage should be held together, that may sometimes mean that no act of intercourse within marriage should preclude the possibility of procreation, and that no act of procreation should be performed independently of the physical intercourse of the partners. Though this view has certainly been held, and probably still is held, within some Christian churches, it is not generally accepted by Anglicans. Anglicans usually hold that love may be expressed through sexual intercourse even when the use of contraceptives prevents the possibility of procreation, and that it is quite proper to plan both the number and timing of children within a marriage. Thus, although one may be unwilling to say that it is entirely up to the partners whether

to have children or not within a proper Christian marriage, one may certainly say that they may plan the number of children by the use of contraceptive techniques. This means, of course, that an element of conscious responsible planning necessarily enters into the matter of procreation. It therefore becomes impossible to say that the procreational and relational goods of marriage must be held together on every occasion, or even on most occasions since, after the wanted number of children has been achieved, one may use contraceptives on all subsequent occasions.

108. Is there any way, then, in which we may say that these goods are held together? One may say that the procreation of children is not just an optional matter of choice for Christians. It is a proper good of marriage, intended by the ordinance of the Creator himself. It is one of the proper purposes of marriage. So, except for very good reasons, every Christian marriage should seek to fulfil itself by the procreation of children. And such procreation should not take place outside the marriage bond. Similarly, that mutual companionship, help and comfort, for better or worse, which the couple promise at their marriage to give and accept one from the other, is not some sort of optional extra to marriage. It, too, is a proper good, ordained by God. Its proper locus is marriage. In saying that these goods should be held together, one may be saying that the intention to have children – even when it is responsibly planned, and therefore very much brought under human control – and the intention to maintain lifelong fidelity, for better or worse, should positively interrelate. Each should strengthen and support the other. One may go further and say that even where family planning is used, the partners are to accept a child as a gift within their marriage (including children conceived 'by mistake'). And the mutual relationship should be widened to include love for children of the marriage. In other words, the important points are: that procreation should not occur entirely outside the loving relationship; and that the loving relationship should issue in the good of children, unless there are strong reasons to the contrary (like genetic defect of a grave kind).

109. If it is agreed that the procreational and relational goods of marriage are sufficiently held together in the marriage as a whole, and that therefore contraception is not destructive of this, a further question must be asked concerning the permissibility of the use of technical procedures which do not involve any relational good (i.e. there is no physical intercourse, even less a strong and enduring union, between the genetic

procreators). The issue will scarcely arise for those who have already accepted that intercourse may properly take place without leaving open the possibility of procreation. For they are already committed to the permissibility – and indeed the desirability of sundering procreative and relationship acts in particular cases; and not just in a few particular cases, as we have seen, but in the vast majority. There is clearly no barrier for them to using an artificial technique of procreation, as long as such techniques are not used entirely outside the context of a loving relationship. Now in such cases, the technique is offered as an aid to the restoration of a good proper to the marriage, which through some handicap has been impeded. So it is calculated to strengthen the relational good, and the bond between the various goods which go together to make a proper Christian marriage. It seems, then, that the use of assisted fertilisation by a couple who cannot, or who are advised on medical grounds, not to have children is acceptable, since it may be said to hold together the procreational and relational goods within the marriage as a whole. (Further questions are raised by IVF which are concerned with the question of experimentation on embryos (see the argument of Chapter 3).)

110. It is thought that we may be attempting to achieve a mastery over human nature itself, possibly involving a reduction of it to the status of an object to be made and manipulated, in encouraging a technological way of thinking about procreation. The natural processes embody and express much larger patterns and relationships on which our whole experience of the world and each other depends. It is clearly possible for a mature and thoughtful couple to use a technical procedure in procreation without coming to think any differently about each other and about their children than they would otherwise have done. What is feared is the impact on our culture of a technological way of thinking about sexual intercourse and procreation. Those who feel this strongly will be reluctant to embark on such a procedure. They feel that sexual intercourse forms the centre of a network of instinctive family relationships which is complex and deep-rooted, and that nothing should be countenanced which threatens this complex network. They will feel that it is in sexual intercourse that we serve all three goods of marriage at once. It is there supremely that we not only engender children, we not only delight in our partners, we not only experience the disciplined direction of our instincts, but we do all these things together and at once. Here we grasp the multivalent structure of

marriage immediately, and our attitudes to partner and children are formed accordingly.

111. A Christian couple may decide that, if it is permissible to plan responsibly the number and timing of children, by the use of contraceptives, then we are already seeking and achieving a greater mastery over the processes of reproduction without reducing anything to the status of an object. They will know that it is not true that in each act of sexual intercourse they engender children as well as delighting in each other. They may therefore conclude, having carefully and prayerfully considered the risks and alternatives such as adoption, that they are right, in situations where they are not otherwise able to have children of their own, to engender children by appropriate artificial means, within the context of their own loving relationship. They will certainly wish to guard against any undermining of commitment to the goods of marriage which, they believe, have been willed by God himself. Yet the responsible use of IVF to remove the disability of childlessness within marriage will not threaten to undermine the interweaving of procreational and relational goods in general within marriage. In fact, in specific marriages, it may offer an enrichment of the marriage relationship which both partners gladly accept.

112. The situation is significantly different when we come to consider DI. For here there is a question of introducing genetic material from outside the union altogether. What, then, is left of the procreative end of the marriage? Simply the parental nurture of the child, beginning with the pregnancy and birth. One parent makes a genetic, and usually gestatory contribution to the child, but the other does not. So here procreation is separated from relationship completely at the genetic level, even though the connection between the two is preserved at the social level. In attempting to assess how serious an objection this poses to the practice of gamete donation, we may first consider two contrasting ways in which the practice is sometimes described, even though these descriptions are inaccurate and misleading.

113. Gamete donation is sometimes described as a form of adoption, sometimes as a form of adultery. It resembles adoption in that the parents accept the child voluntarily, although they are not its genetic parents. But of course in DI the parents take on a much more consciously responsible role. They do not decide to nurture a child who already exists. They decide

to bring a child into existence who will be genetically only partly their own. Moreover, in English law, the adopted child has the right to know its genetic parents, under certain carefully phased conditions. In DI this is not the case. Upon reaching the age of 18 years the individual may obtain from the HFEA certain non-identifying information about his/her donor i.e. genetic parent. Is it right or wrong to decide to bring a child into being who will not know half its genetic origin? It is true that many children will not know their genetic origins in any case, but that does not resolve the moral problem of whether that is desirable. There will be a difference of view here between those who think that the genetic origins of a child are fundamentally important and those who believe that what is more important is the loving nurture of the child in a stable marital relationship. The authors of this report, though they are all sensitive to this problem, cannot agree on the moral status of the free decision to bring a child into being with the assistance of donated gametes. There are two differing points of view held among us. One is that if donation takes place within a stable marital relationship, it still has the status of a good, though not, of course, one which should become a norm; the other believes that the perils to marriage, as understood by Christians, are so grave that the extension of gamete donation should be strongly discouraged, and DI dislodged from the established position it now holds among the techniques of aided fertilisation.

114.   DI may be compared to adultery insofar as the presence of the child is founded on a genetic union that is extrinsic to the family. Of course, there is no offence against the married partner, there is no breaking of the relationship of physical fidelity and there is no real relationship with a person outside the marriage. It is certainly quite unlike the physical act of adultery therefore.[2] But the parents have still decided to bring into being a child who is not genetically their own, and which does involve the procreative (even if anonymous) activity of another human being. Is it right or wrong to decide to bring into being a child who is not genetically the offspring of the partners concerned in the decision? We are conscious that Anglican tradition hitherto has opposed the donation of genetic material.[3] However, it is right to reflect again on the adequacy of statements about this in the light of further knowledge and experience. Bearing in mind that we are only considering cases where marriages are deprived of the good of children, what we are asking is whether this defect can be remedied by the

use of genetic material from outside the marriage. We differ on this, depending on whether we see the genetic as the most basic manifestation of the personal and find the alienation of genetic parenthood from marriage a development which undermines the Christian understanding; or whether we judge that, although everyone is fundamentally influenced and limited by his or her genetic endowment, nevertheless the overriding factor is the social context which can assure proper love, respect and care. To this extent the question of genetic origin is not of fundamental moral importance, when compared with the question of how the child will be loved and cared for.[4]

115.   Another concern is that the extension of human decision-making about procreation beyond the genetic confines of the married couple introduces an element of dominion over nature which appears unjustifiable to some and possibly even threatening to human values. But to others it is little more than an extension of that responsible control over procreation which contraception already has introduced. Though there may be dangers in human control of procreation, they are unlikely to be realised in these very limited and carefully controlled situations, so that what is required is the existence of safeguards to the procedure, rather than its prohibition. Even if some feel personally uneasy about the use of DI, they may not wish to prohibit its use in law, by those who conscientiously feel that it may strengthen the marriage bond and remedy the lack of a great and natural good of marriage.

116.   Family affections stretch back to and embrace pregnancy, during which the bond between mother and child – and, at one remove, between father and child – is emotionally secured. This fact leads us, despite our disagreements on ovum and semen donation, to a common mind on the practice of surrogate motherhood. This term refers, strictly speaking, not to a technological practice (for the technology is the same as that of gamete donation with IVF) but to a contractual or quasi-contractual agreement. The parents, having made their genetic contribution to the fertilisation of the embryo *in vitro*, will assume the duties and privileges of parenthood only after the child has been carried in the womb by another woman. Our view is that the case for ovum donation itself – i.e. for the separation of the female genetic contribution from the mother's gestatory role stands or falls with the claim that the genetic relation is in itself not of decisive importance compared with the gestatory one. But in the case of

surrogate motherhood, it is precisely the gestatory role which is being minimised. To those of us who accept a comparative devaluation of genetic factors on their own, it seems clear that the mother who bears the child has a true parental and, already to some degree, a social role. Thus any subsequent transfer of parental responsibility must be viewed as a form of adoption arrangement. And, while there is nothing wrong with adoption, there is something undesirable about creating children specifically for the purpose of adoption, and even more so, about so creating them for financial consideration. To those of us who in any case regard the genetic contribution as of overriding importance, the separation of the two female contributions to the biological origins of a child appears as in itself unacceptable.

117.   We are in accord, then, that in surrogate motherhood the Christian institution of the family is fundamentally endangered, and thus that it cannot be morally acceptable as a practice for Christians. On other types of gamete donation we are not of one mind, but we would all wish to ensure that such practices were properly controlled and recorded.

118.   Finally, we would wish to reiterate that our fundamental concern in these matters is for the preservation of the good of Christian marriage, as instituted by God himself, and for the welfare of children, who are to be brought up in the fear and love of the Lord.⁵ It will need much observation and discussion before we can come to a clear mind about whether these practices threaten marriage or the true welfare of children, or conversely if they are a blessing in marriage. But it is above all important to recognise the new situation in which we stand, with possibilities now open to us which have never before existed. In this situation, our traditions of moral thought need to be extended and rethought. It may well be that previous ways of thinking will not be sustainable on reflection. On the other hand, we should not give up too lightly positions which have been important to generations of Christians. Our Working Party has contained committed Christians who span a wide range of Anglican moral traditions. We have sought to provide a guide to thinking on these issues which has been rather painfully forged in our own discussions. We believe that it is important to continue to wrestle with these questions.

Footnotes

1   These emphases are different in other traditions. For example, the Book of Common Order of the Church of Scotland lists the goods as 'the lifelong companionship, help and comfort which husband and wife ought to have to each other...the continuance of the holy ordinance of family life...and the welfare of human society'.

2   A case in the Scottish courts has declared that DI is not legally adultery. In Edinburgh in 1958 a Mrs Maclennan successfully defended herself against a charge of adultery by claiming that a child born to her was the result of DI. The judge ruled that physical intercourse was necessary for adultery to take place.

3   See the findings of the Archbishop of Canterbury's Commission in 1948, and the 1959 Memorandum of Evidence submitted on behalf of the Church of England on AID (now DI) to the interdepartmental committee chaired by Lord Feversham.

4   The limited number of studies of children born following DI that have been carried out suggest that they are generally more balanced and healthy children than the average. After all, they have been desired and sought in a way which is not true of some children born of normal intercourse.

5   We consider that there is a continuing need for research into the well-being of children born as a result of the various assisted conception techniques. Only then can it be determined whether the provisions in the HFE Act concerning the welfare of children are adequate. We support the HFEA in encouraging and supporting long-term follow-up studies of families involved in the various assisted conception techniques to ascertain their impact on family life and to gather information concerning the physical and psychosocial development of the children.

5

Conclusions for practice

119. In forming judgements on actual possible practices we must begin by clearing away some basic questions. For example, it might well be asked, 'ought we to treat infertility?' Infertility is an ill preventing married couples entering into the blessing of having their own children. None of the theological arguments and moral considerations set out in this report would discourage the treatment of infertility. That does not mean, however, that every possible treatment for infertility can be justified. We believe that the theological and moral argument is concerned with judging the acceptability of different possible ways of dealing with these real and often painful problems.

120. There are a number of fundamental matters of broad principle on which we are agreed. First, we are committed to the unity of marriage and the integrity of the family as traditionally accepted in the Church. The points on which we differ, which we set out below, concern whether particular practices do or do not, in principle, undermine these Christian understandings. Second, we are committed to the utmost respect for human life. Our differences are not concerned with the protection of human life bearing the image of God, but with whether the human embryo in its very early days of development possesses this status and thus has a right to such protection. Third, we believe that the principle of consent, as set out in Chapter 2, both in relation to research and also in relation to the provision of infertility services, is of basic importance. Free and informed consent is required from any human being who may be the subject of research. That consent may not extend to the threat of actual physical harm. Whatever judgements we form on different methods of resolving infertility we believe that the free and informed consent of all the parties is basic to the procedure. These matters have been discussed at greater length elsewhere in this report. We draw attention to them because they are basic principles by which we must judge the acceptability of the procedures involved both in therapy and in research.

Technologies for resolving infertility

Enabling natural fertilisation

121. A great deal of work done which is aimed at resolving the problems of infertility succeeds in enabling couples, who otherwise would not be able to do so, to have children of their own. Work done, for example, in reconstructing a woman's tubes is one such technology. These are welcome developments.

Artificial insemination by husband

122. AIH is a practice in which human intervention is assisting the natural process and enabling it to reach its desired fulfilment. We view this as an aid to a couple in having a child of their own and thereby forming a natural family. We have no difficulty in supporting the intention of the act, the nature of the act, and its consequences. We recognise that the practice interferes with the course of nature and that it separates procreation from the act of intercourse. However, the Church of England permits the practice of artificial contraception within marriage which likewise interferes with the course of nature and which prevents procreation arising from the act of intercourse. Approval of AIH would seem to follow naturally from the Church of England's stance on contraception.

In vitro fertilisation

123. In *principle* a similar argument applies to this technique where the egg is that of the genetic mother and the sperm that of the genetic father and where, after fertilisation has taken place outside the womb, the embryo is implanted into the mother's womb. Thus a couple are enabled to have a natural family of their own. Some of us, however, are not able to support IVF in practice. This is because the practice is inextricably bound up with research and usually involves the creation of more embryos than will be used to resolve the problem of infertility. The moral problem is seen in the search to render pregnancy as nearly certain as may be. It is symptomatic, it is argued, of the easy way in which technical intervention moves from assisting the natural process to seeking to improve it. Others of us do not share these difficulties and view the procedure as a legitimate way of enabling married couples to enter into the blessing of family life through having children of their own.

Enabling fertilisation through the use of donor gametes

124. The involvement of third parties who donate sperm or ova to be used to enable fertilisation for couples who otherwise are not able to bear children adds new dimensions to the moral argument. Here we have to acknowledge that the different traditions we have sought to outline in Chapter 4 lead to different conclusions about the practice.

Donor insemination

125. DI introduces a third party into the intimacies of married life in the form of donated sperm in cases where the husband's own sperm is unable to succeed in fertilising the ovum of the wife. Marriage is the union of one man and one woman for life. The Memorandum of Evidence submitted on this issue in 1959 on behalf of the Church of England reaffirmed the findings of the Archbishop of Canterbury's Commission of 1948 that, 'artificial insemination with donated semen involves a breach of the marriage. It violates the exclusive union set up between husband and wife' (no.3, p.58). There are two opinions among us on this. There are those who hold that when a couple become 'one flesh' in marriage they belong to one another in such a close and exclusive way that nothing and no one else should take their place in sexual union and in the procreation that results from it. Union and procreation are indissolubly linked. Others, however, believing that a proper development of Anglican ethical thought on these matters is both possible and desirable (cf. the evolution of Anglican thinking on contraception), affirm that it is possible for a couple to hold in good conscience that the semen of a third party imports nothing alien into the marriage relationship and does not adulterate it as physical union would. It is a possible view of the exclusiveness of the marital relationship that it concerns physical congress rather than the giving and reception of semen which is its normal accompaniment.

126. We would also wish to affirm the importance of clarity and truthfulness in these matters and that any use of the practice which involves deceit about the genetic identity of the child so brought into the world is offensive to Christian values.

Egg donation

127. We are not agreed as to whether this practice is in principle the same as in DI and therefore involves no fundamentally new moral dilemmas (which would mean that similar arguments to those used to conclude that DI is permissible in the light of Christian principles would be applied to this practice) or whether it raises additional ethical problems. These are seen as three distinct features of egg donation:

(i) The woman bears a child who is not genetically related to her. The child has three parents and this is a basic confusion of the Christian understanding of parenthood. However a child resulting from DI also has three parents.

(ii) While DI takes place *in vivo*, egg donation takes place *in vitro* and thereby raises some of the arguments used to question IVF.

(iii) Medical intervention is required to recover the egg and there is some slight risk to the donor.

Embryo donation

128. In this practice an embryo fertilised *in vitro* by the use of donated ovum and sperm is implanted into the womb of the woman of a couple who are to be its social parents. In this way couples where both the woman is unable to produce an egg and the man is infertile are able to have a family.

Permissible intervention

129. Nature is God-given, but is flawed. Human beings are called to co-operate with God in treating and (so far as possible) remedying any natural deficiency. We gratefully acknowledge the blessings that come from a right use of medical technology to assist a couple in founding a family. In considering embryo donation we have had to determine the boundaries beyond which we should not transgress in altering the course of nature. We have found here, as we have experienced elsewhere, a theological division concerning the extent to which nature is given by God with its ends determined, and the extent to which we may regard it as 'raw material' to fashion for our own good ends. Some would argue, particu-

larly in the case of embryo donation, that technological interference with the course of nature goes far beyond the remedying of a natural defect. They believe that the fertilisation of an ovum by artificial means from an anonymous donor, to be implanted in a mother and reared by parents who have no genetic relationship with the child, entails treating that child too much as a product. Opponents of the practice fear that knowledge about his or her totally anonymous origins might have a deleterious effect on a person born in this way. Nevertheless, the distinction between implanting an embryo with a donated ovum, one with donated semen, and one where both ovum and semen are donated, seems one of degree. Once the principle of donation is granted, some would see little reason to insist that at least 50 per cent of the embryo's genes should be those of one social parent. When genetic and social parentage have been sundered in principle, it seems an uneasy compromise to try to reaffirm a partial link between the two.

Surrogacy and womb-leasing

130.   Surrogacy involves a contract (which may or may not involve financial considerations) between a woman who will bear a child to be handed over at birth and a couple who will then be its parents. It is, therefore, a broader question involving considerations other than the medical one concerned with resolving infertility. The moral arguments used against donation and IVF involving donation apply here. The unique features of surrogacy, however, lead those who would support the use of donated gametes to enable couples to have children they otherwise would not be able to have, to question surrogacy on practical and moral grounds. The practical and moral problems are multiple and involve a confused complexity of relationships which we do not believe it is possible to resolve at present. Strong bonding, for example, takes place between a woman and the child she bears in her womb and this may lead to her being unwilling to let the child go to the contracting couple after birth. Moreover we believe that this practice, especially where it involves the payment of money for this service, is undermining the dignity of women in the bearing of children they have no intention of mothering.

Secondary effects of these practices

Spare embryos

131.   IVF usually involves the production of more embryos than are needed to resolve the problems of infertility. This raises a number of questions. First, there is the question of whether embryos should be produced where there is no intention of allowing them to develop. The judgement formed on this depends, at least in part, on the judgement made about the status of the early embryo. The arguments on this have been set out in Chapter 3 and further comment on the differing judgements is made in the section of this chapter concerned with research (Paragraph 136ff).

132.   Second, there are questions concerning what may be done with such spare embryos. Some may be frozen with a view to keeping them for further pregnancies, thereby enabling infertile couples to enlarge their family without further hormonal or surgical intervention. To some, this so removes the natural contingencies of conception and the creation of a family that they regard it as an attempt at improving rather than assisting nature. Others believe that, provided it is possible to deal satisfactorily with questions of ownership and control, no fundamental moral principles have been breached in this practice.

133.   What may we do, however, with spare embryos which are not going to be implanted and allowed to develop? Acknowledging that this fact in itself raises moral problems for some, the question remains whether (and how) they should be disposed of or made available for research which would also involve eventual disposal. The answer to these questions again lies, at least in part, in the judgement to be formed about the nature and status of the embryo in its early days. It also involves a judgement about whether the respect which all of us believe is due to all human life, leads to the rejection of any research involving the use and disposal of human life. Before we turn to these questions one further matter is worthy of comment.

134.   Another possible effect of the developments in these areas involves their potentiality for genetic selection. For example, how are we to react to the possibility of being able to select the sex of our children? Some see this as such interference with nature that it takes away something basic to God's intention, namely the delight experienced in the contingencies of

procreation. The sex of our children is something to be received by us, not to be determined by us. Others do not share that moral anxiety and, again, provided it is possible to organise and manage such choices in an acceptable manner, see no basic moral problems with it.[1]

135.   However, the possibilities of genetic choice in the future may go much further. Any attempt at the positive selecting of personality or aesthetic traits (even if it is ever technically possible, which many professionals deny) raises fundamental questions about the sovereignty of God. It endangers the sense of wonder we feel in all the rich range of individuality. We are not oppressed by the prospect of such developments, because the image of God which makes us fully human is immutable and undefileable. Notwithstanding, we believe that seeking to determine what sort of people we wish to have is in conflict with our responsibility to God for our stewardship of our life and our world.

Research

136.   The judgements formed on the issues raised in Chapter 3 about the status of the embryo and about the extent and limits of human dominion as set out in Chapter 2 form the background to any discussions on research which uses human embryos.

137.   We are not able to agree on the status of the human embryo in its early development. One view holds that human life from conception is a continuum and should be afforded the status and protection we give to all human beings. It is therefore difficult to see how consent could be given, even by proxy, for research to be undertaken on human embryos at any stage which would involve their hurt and destruction. The other view holds that we have a duty to judge when, in the development of human life, a particular life has reached a stage where it possesses the essential features of the full human being and therefore must be protected. Those of us who take this second view would wish to be cautious about affording protection at an earlier, rather than later, stage. In principle, research could only be permitted before that stage had been reached. In the Response which the Board for Social Responsibility made to the Government on the Warnock Committee Report in 1984 the majority view was that this occurred with the completion of the period of individuation by 14 days.

138.   The question, however, is broader than this. Even if we judge that it is not possible to afford an embryo equal protection to other human beings in the first 14 days of its life, we may still judge that respect for human life puts a boundary around the embryo, protecting it from that exercise of human dominion which threatens its existence. Again, we are not agreed on this. Some would wish to affirm that the good which is to be achieved by permitting research may be a stronger principle and therefore more important than any disrespect it may involve for human life. But even though the end may be judged good the means may be unacceptable.

139.   This leads to the further question that even if research can, in principle, be permitted to what ends can it be directed? Here we are agreed that if research is permissible it is only permissible for the good end of seeking to resolve the problems of infertility and genetic disorder. Research for other goals is not acceptable. We would view with concern, for instance, any suggestion that human embryos might be used for monitoring the effects of new chemical compounds.

140.   That is only one aspect of the question 'what are the boundaries for research?'. These boundaries touch not only upon purposes but also upon the status of the embryo. This defines the point at which we draw a line and agree that the breach of it would involve research on human beings without their full and informed consent.

141.   Is it permissible to produce embryos for research purposes? Some would argue that embryos ought to be produced only for the purpose of implantation and development into full human beings. For reasons already indicated, this argument is not accepted as binding by all understandings of the Christian tradition. There are further arguments which relate to the sphere of social morality and they involve judgements about whether society possesses the maturity as well as the means for restricting research work within acceptable bounds of objectives and practice. To accept the principle that it is possible to consider producing embryos for research does not necessarily mean that it is right to do it in every given set of circumstances.

142.   Even where it is agreed that the production of embryos for research is unacceptable, the question remains whether research may be permitted on embryos produced to remedy infertility and are then not needed once

the problems have successfully been resolved. The only point here, in addition to those already discussed, concerns the judgement to be made whether it is better to make use of these embryos for good ends in seeking to find ways to resolve infertility problems and problems of genetic disorder or whether it is better (or the lesser evil) to dispose of them as reverently as possible.

In conclusion

143. We have tried to show how Christians, who are seeking to respond to developments in human knowledge in the light of a desire to be faithful to Christian tradition, might approach these complex subjects. We hope that what we have done will enable others to make their judgements and encourage the Church to continue to explore these matters out of a desire to possess the mind of Christ on these issues.

Footnotes

1   BSR (1993). *Response to the Human Fertilisation and Embryology Authority's Public Consultation Document on Sex Selection.*

6

Questions concerning pastoral care

144.   Matters affecting fertility and parenthood raise very deep personal feelings in people. It is not always easy to help people talk about these matters in a way which helps them arrive at responsible understandings and social decisions. Infertility is often hard to bear. It can lead to feelings of personal inadequacy and place very real strains upon a marriage. It is one thing to choose not to have a family. It is quite another for a couple to want to have children of their own but not to be able to do so. It is important to understand the helplessness some couples feel when they have done all the right things and still not conceived. At times when couples feel the loss there is the temptation for one party to sense their own inadequacy – it is his or her 'fault' – whilst the other resents their partner's incapacity to enable their union to issue in children. On top of this couples can sense social disapproval for their childlessness. Their own parents and the members of their community can appear to be pressing them to be 'normal' and start a family of their own. In the Biblical story of Abraham and Sarah we can see the harmful effect of living with childlessness and the consequent joy and fulfilment when a child eventually came to the marriage. A mixture of personal emotions, social expectations and cultural norms serve to underscore the difficulty of living with infertility. It is important to remember that a couple may have experienced considerable distress before they arrive at the point of seeking help.

145.   To the needs of those who may look for some resolution of their problems from contemporary fertilisation techniques, we must add the needs of those who work in this area. Those involved both in research and in offering therapeutic help have impressed upon us their need for support in responding to the ethical and pastoral dilemmas involved in their work. The Church ought not to forget the need for good pastoral care of those who have a professional commitment to work on these issues. Careful work on the moral issues needs to be made available to people involved in pastoral care.

146. The first hurdle to be overcome in enabling pastoral care to begin is that of making contact both with people who live with the dilemmas of infertility and who may be considering seeking help through using human fertilisation techniques, and with people whose professional work is in these areas. It is often hard enough for couples to be open about their problems to themselves. If the Church, therefore, presents a rigid and negative face to them it is very unlikely that they will ever pluck up courage to seek advice and pastoral counsel from its members. Whatever judgement we make of the complex moral questions we need to do so in clear sensitivity and sympathy for those directly affected.

147. The needs of people seeking pastoral support will vary not only according to their own personal reactions and experience but also according to the quality of service offered to them by any agencies with which they may be in touch or considering approaching. The HFE Act recognises the importance of this aspect for it states that 'A woman shall not be provided with any treatment services... unless the woman being treated, and, where she is being treated together with a man, the man have been given a suitable opportunity to receive proper counselling about the implications of taking the proposed steps and have been provided with such relevant information as is proper.' The HFEA Code of Practice gives detailed instructions as to how this should be carried out.

148. One of the important areas of concern for the churches is the acknowledgement that this is not just a medical problem but one involving deep personal issues about sex, and about relationships inside a marriage and within a family. This point is made with some force in a report from the Australian Anglican Church's Social Responsibility Commission, *Making Babies – the Test Tube and Christian Ethics* (Canberra: Acorn Press, 1984). After pointing out the seriousness of the possible introduction of third and fourth party gametes into a marriage in order that children can be produced they say:

> In all these circumstances, assuming that all these procedures become approved and go ahead...counselling becomes an absolute essential. This counselling must be not only about the genetic and medical questions, but also about the strength of the marriage relationship, the identity of the child, and the sense of belonging together in the future family unit'. (p. 70)

149.   It is important that such counselling is available to people both before they make use of these techniques and also afterwards in the period of the establishment of the family. This is the pattern now used in adoption practice. The issues concerning building families are no less serious than the techniques of IVF and need a similar and appropriate level of professional counselling input.

150.   It is possible that couples may seek pastoral counsel from the Church. This could make difficult demands on clergy and others especially if they do not have easy access to people with professional skills who might offer support.

151.   The rest of this report discusses the moral questions in the light of this situation. A grasp of these questions is basic to making proper use of pastoral conversation which will need to cover the following areas.

Infertility and childlessness

152.   Infertility places strains upon marriages. Part of the problem lies in the feeling that married couples ought to have children of their own if they are of an age for childbearing. One of the most important ways of providing some resolution of these needs in the past was for childless couples to adopt children. In recent times adoption theory and practice has moved away from any thought that adoption is primarily aimed at resolving the problems of childless couples. The needs of the child to be placed are paramount. This has gone hand in hand with social changes which have resulted in there being very few suitable babies available for adoption. There are many more couples seeking children to adopt than there are babies available. A lot of contemporary adoption work concerns home-finding for groups of children whose needs may not be able to be met by relatively young childless couples – older children in care, mentally and physically handicapped children, and emotionally disturbed children. This leaves many couples unable to have children of their own naturally or by adoption. In the face of feelings of inadequacy and of marital stress it is important to reassure couples that childlessness is not, according to Anglican belief, a threat to the integrity of marriage. A marriage in which there are no children is not in any sense made invalid or reduced to some second-class status. Children are a blessing on marriage. They are not essential to it. Even if it is believed, as some Christians do, that a com-

mitment to marriage implicitly involves a commitment to have children where that is possible, that belief does not question the integrity of those who desire to have children of their own but who cannot. A couple may need reassuring that their sexual relationship in their marriage is valid, God-given, loving and responsible even though children are not conceived. This is important because if couples decide to seek the therapeutic help of modern fertilisation techniques they need to do so out of a considered desire to have a family, not as a way of reinforcing the validity of their marriage in the hope that this will help resolve some of the strains upon it.

153.   In counselling couples who are unable to have children of their own it is important to bear in mind particular points in their experience. For example, where couples are unable to have children it is predominantly the woman who seeks professional help. Yet in around 40 per cent of cases it is the man who is infertile. This suggests that men have difficulty in coming to terms with infertility, and pastoral care may need to take account of this. It is also worth bearing in mind how daunting and discouraging it can be to couples when seeking help to be faced with the routines of infertility clinics involving the giving of endless personal histories to doctors, and the requirement to masturbate to order. Some clinics are more sensitive than others. It can be very humiliating for a couple.

Marriage

154.   We have already indicated that we see no fundamental moral problems in the use of IVF to enable couples to have children of their own. The moral problems concern the acceptability of research on human embryos (which is needed to improve the practice) and the loss of embryonic life in the disposal of spare embryos. Our moral discussion has centred upon the questions raised by the introduction of third and/or fourth-party material (donated sperm and ova). Here we have discussed questions concerning whether such donation in principle disrupts the union of a marriage. It is important that couples are helped to explore these questions of principle as well as to consider their own personal reactions to having children who may not be theirs genetically at all, or may only be genetically related to one of the partners. It requires strength in the marriage and a maturity in relationships to be able to do this and to discover a deepening bond in

their relationship as a result. Hardly any research has been done on the effects on the family of DI and IVF. Couples have found that having a family by such means has enriched their marriage. It is often asserted, however, that it could lead to stress, especially where there is a lack of openness about what is being done; there is a need for factual information on this subject. The needs of a couple, let alone those of the child, require understanding about what is proposed and about what this means for the development of their family.

Family

155.   From long experience we know that many people are able to offer parental love and commitment to children who are genetically not their own. The bonds of love in the family are experienced by all who form the social family. Couples who adopt children usually succeed in creating healthy families in which every member is able to experience love, security and growth. The same can be true for families formed by the help of new technologies. Such experience, however, is not assisted by confusion. In the case of families made up of members who came to their life by means of human fertilisation using third-party gametes, clarity about how the family came to be is important to its chance of success. Clarity is important not only for the relationship of the parents to each other but also for the other relationships in the family – parent and child, child to child, and child to the extended family and wider community. Openness is essential to the child's sense of being wanted in the family. Pretending that things are not as they are can mean that the parents are not fully reconciled either to the reasons for seeking such help or to the means themselves. Children can read into that a sense that their status in the family is ambivalent and that in some way they are not fully wanted or accepted. Pastoral care involves talk about healthy attitudes in the family.

156.   Some of the problems can reside in the attitudes of close family and friends and it may be that they will need help and support in managing and contributing to the whole climate in the family. Potential grandparents may find these matters very hard to understand and accept.

Identity

157.   All of this goes closely with the insistence elsewhere in this report that the procedures allow for clarity about the identity of the child. Our genetic life is part of what it means to be human and children are entitled, therefore, to a clear understanding of their own origins and how they came to be the people they are in the family they are part of. The Australian report referred to previously puts it like this:

> An essential ingredient in any family which is going to sur-
> vive under all contemporary pressures is openness and
> frankness. Any secrecy about a child's procreation or biolog-
> ical origin produces stress not only in the early years, but on
> a continuing basis if the secret is going to be kept. The stress
> is worse if adults in the family circle know the secret, but the
> child does not'. (p. 71)

158.   The same point is made in the British Agencies for Adoption and Fostering (BAAF) booklet, AID *and After*, where note is taken of the wide research done into adoption indicating the importance of openness and honesty. The point is not only that secrecy in the family on such matters is potentially damaging and could be explosive, it is also the simple moral imperative that an individual person has a right to know about their own life and origins. The difficulties adults may have in articulating the truth must not be allowed to override the needs and care of children. The atti-tudes potential parents hold to these sorts of questions are a crucial part of pastoral discussion.

Human life

159.   Some human fertilisation techniques require the deliberate dis-posal of human embryos. Christians are not agreed about the moral judgements to be made on this. Some regard it as inadmissible, others countenance it if it is necessary for the greater good of bringing a child into the world, others still are not unduly concerned about the loss of embryos at such an early stage. It is hoped that future research may reduce the need for the deliberate destruction of embryos. Lack of agreement on the morality of embryo disposal, however, ought not to prevent pastoral work to help Christians consider their reactions to these facts. In making

their decisions about what to do, couples need to know what is involved if they decide to have a child by IVF. There can sometimes be a temptation for practitioners and pastors to suppress moral discussion out of a natural desire to enable needs to be met. The extent to which people can respond to even the hardest moral dilemmas is an indication of their maturity to live with the decisions they make in these matters. These matters need handling sensitively rather than sensationally or adversarily. People should be aware of all the main implications of what they propose when they make their decision.

Other people

160. The highly personal character of sex and reproduction tends to make people see them as private matters concerning the couple and their future family. In raising questions about what happens if the marriage eventually breaks down, BAAF reminds us that these matters are not entirely private even though they may seem to be:

> Although it may seem reasonable to advise a couple to keep this matter entirely private, couples are not entirely private individuals. They are members of families and have relationships with other adults. If the marriage into which an AID (DI) child is born breaks down and the mother's new husband has children from his first marriage, new and complex family relationships will result. (AID *and After*, p. 23)

161. Decisions in this area involve others – the donors who offer the seed of their own life, those who offer professional help, the wider family, and the wider community whose understanding of family experience is affected by what we choose to do at a personal level. People need to be helped to make their choices in the knowledge of their responsibilities to consider all who have an interest in their decision.

162. Good pastoral care helps to clarify issues and prepare the way for people to make responsible decisions. It requires sensitivity, skill in counselling, insight into the issues raised and a capacity to work on the moral questions. Such work can only serve to deepen all our understandings of the mind of Christ in these matters.

Appendix I

Evidence and reports

The Working Party met with the following to take oral evidence and to discuss the issues raised:

The Most Revd and Rt Hon. John Stapylton Habgood, then Archbishop of York;

The Very Revd Peter Baelz, then Dean of Durham;

Professor Gordon Stirrat, Professor of Obstetrics & Gynaecology, University of Bristol;

The Revd Canon Professor Gordon Dunstan, Professor Emeritus of Moral and Social Theology, University of London;

Professor Robert Edwards, Department of Physiology, University of Cambridge;

The Revd Canon Professor Anthony Dyson, Professor of Social and Pastoral Theology, University of Manchester.

The Working Party noted the submissions made to the Warnock Committee of Inquiry into Human Fertilisation and Embryology by the following bodies:

The Catholic Bishops of Great Britain;

The Church of England Children's Society;

Family Forum;

The Family Law Committee of the Law Society;

The Medical Research Council;

The Mothers' Union;

Nationwide Festival of Light;

The Royal College of Obstetricians and Gynaecologists;

The Royal Society;

The Social Welfare Commission of the Catholic Bishops' Conference (England and Wales).

The Working Party also took note of the following:

The Report of the Royal College of Obstetricians & Gynaecologists on *In Vitro Fertilisation and Embryology: Replacement or Transfer*;

The British Agencies for Adoption and Fostering paper AID *and After* (1984);

The publication at the request of the Australian Anglican Church's Social Responsibility Commission *Making Babies.*

Appendix II

Background literature

Berry, A. C. (1993). *Beginnings*. London: Christian Medical Fellowship.

Boyd, K., Callaghan, B. & Shotter, E. (1986). *Life Before Birth:Consensus in Medical Ethics*. London: SPCK.

British Agencies for Adoption & Fostering (1984). *AID and After*. London: BAAF.

Bromham, D. R., Dalton, M. E., Jackson, J. C. & Millican, P. J. R. (eds) (1992). *Ethics in Reproductive Medicine*. London: Springer-Verlag.

Carter, C. O. (ed) (1983). *Developments in Human Reproduction and their Eugenic, Ethical Implications*. London: Academic Press.

Comment on Reproductive Ethics (CORE) (1995). *The Human Fertilisation and Embryology Authority: A Critique of its First Reports (1992–1994)*. London: Centre for Bioethics and Public Policy.

Congregation for the Doctrine of the Faith (1987). *Donum Vitae* (Instructions on Respect for Human Life in its Origins). English translation, London: Catholic Truth Society.

Cooke, J. (1985). *Why Us Lord? The Trauma of Infertility: Personal Experience*. Basingstoke: Pickering & Inglis.

Coughlan, M. J. (1990). *The Vatican, the Law and the Human Embryo*. Basingstoke: Macmillan.

Council for Science & Society (1984). *Human Procreation. New Developments in Human Reproduction*. London: CSS.

Dunstan, G. R. & Seller, M. J. (eds) (1988). *The Status of the Human Embryo: Perspectives from Moral Tradition*. London & Oxford: King Edward's Hospital Fund for London & Oxford University Press.

Dyson, A. & Harris, J. (eds) (1990). *Experiments on Embryos*. London: Routledge.

Dyson, A. (1995). *The Ethics of IVF*. London: Mowbray.

Edwards, R. G. & Purdy, J. (eds) (1982). *Human Conception In Vitro*. London: Academic.

Edwards, R. G. & Steptoe, P. (1980). *A Matter of Life*. London: Hutchinson.

Fishel, S. & Symonds, E. M. (eds) (1986). *In Vitro Fertilisation: Past, Present, Future*. Oxford and Washington DC: IRL Press.

Ford, N. M. (1988). *When Did I Begin?* Cambridge: Cambridge University Press.

Free Church Federal Council/British Council of Churches (1982). *Choices in Childlessness*. London: FCFC.

Glover, J. (1984). *What Sort of People Should There Be?* Harmondsworth: Pelican.

Gunning, J. & English, V. (1993). *Human In Vitro Fertilization: A Case Study in the Regulation of Medical Innovation*. Aldershot: Dartmouth.

Harris, J. (1993). *Wonderwoman and Superman*. Oxford: Oxford University Press.

Houghton, D. & Houghton, P. (1984). *Coping with Childlessness*. London: Allen & Unwin.

Iglesias, T. (1990). *IVF and Justice*. London: Linacre Centre.

Ison, D. (1983). *Artificial Insemination by Donor*. Nottingham: Grove.

John Paul II. (1995). *Evangelium Vitae* (Encyclical Letter on the Value and Inviolability of Human Life). English translation, London: Catholic Truth Society.

Jones, A. & Bodmer, W.F. (1974). *Our Future Inheritance: Choice or Chance?* Oxford: Oxford University Press.

Jones, D. G. (1984). *Brave New People: Ethical Issues at the Commencement of Life*. Leicester: IVP.

Jones, D. G. (1987). *Manufacturing Humans: The Challenge of the New Reproductive Technologies*. Leicester: IVP.

Mahoney, J. (1984). *Bioethics and Belief*. London: Sheed & Ward.

O'Donovan, O. (1973). *The Christian and the Unborn Child*. Nottingham: Grove.

O'Donovan, O. (1984). *Begotten or Made?* Oxford: Oxford University Press.

Ramsey, P. (1975). *The Ethics of Fetal Research*. New Haven & London: Yale University Press.

Reichenbach, B. R. & Anderson, V. E. (1995). *On Behalf of God*. Grand Rapids: Erdmans.

Singer, P., Kuhse, H., Buckle, S., Kasimba, P. (eds) (1990). *Embryo Experimentation*. Cambridge: Cambridge University Press.

Singer, P. & Wells, D. (1984). *The Reproduction Revolution: New Ways of Making Babies*. Oxford: Oxford University Press.

Snowden, R. & Mitchell, G. D. (1981). *The Artificial Family: A Consideration of Artificial Insemination by Donor*. London: Allen & Unwin.

Snowden, R., Mitchell, G. D. & Snowden, E. M. (1983). *Artificial Reproduction: A Social Investigation*. London: Allen & Unwin.

The Ciba Foundation (1986). *Embryo Research: Yes or No?* London: Tavistock Publications.

Torrance, T. F. (1984). *Test-Tube Babies: Morals, Science and the Law*. Edinburgh: Scottish Academic Press.

The Human Fertilisation & Embryology Authority produces Annual Reports and a regularly updated Code of Practice. These can be obtained from the Authority at Paxton House, 30 Artillery Lane, London E1 7LS.